PRAISE FOR

VERY RECENT HISTORY

"[The] most hilarious satire of the summer. . . . A brave new amalgam of reportage and story. . . . Takes on the hyperreal gloss of an *E! True Hollywood Story*, narrated as though by some earnest alien sociologist from the future."

—*GQ*

"In the tradition of Janet Malcolm, Renata Adler, and Joan Didion, but with a style and wit all his own, Choire Sicha has performed a useful public service: he has described how sex, love, work, and money function for young people in the wake of a financial crisis that quietly eliminated the last remnants of their city's idea of itself. This book will be especially useful for the generation it describes, who are so caught up in an infinite now that they risk forgetting, and repeating, slightly less recent history."

—Emily Gould, author of *And the Heart Says Whatever*

"Sicha's position as a journalist is so impressively embedded, it could be described as vascular. . . . A Vonnegut-esque manual of the era for future aliens interested in life in that lost empire known as twenty-first-century America."

—*Interview*

"An exemplary entry in—and in many ways a blistering critique of—a style of writing I think of as post-fiction. This writing represents a chiasmus between the real and the made up, blurring the two into nonrecognition."

—Michael H. Miller, *New York Observer*

"Sicha's detached prose . . . makes that year feel more absurd than any of us might remember. . . . A fresh look at a seemingly distant world that is actually our own. Grade: A-"

—*Entertainment Weekly*

"Has the same time-capsule charm as a book many of us read and were fascinated by in elementary school, *Motel of the Mysteries*, in which the world was destroyed and future generations were left to wonder at objects like a toilet."

—*Time*

"Choire Sicha's writing charms and delights, but beneath the biting wit and cynicism [he] dares to explore the darker underbelly of human avarice and capital [in] a book that's equal parts blindingly terrifying and smartly humorous, and one of the most clever reads I've encountered in a long time."

—NPR

"You look up from the book to find that Sicha took the opportunity to screw a new pair of eyes into your sockets. With his distance and his wit, he's showed you the ridiculousness, and the impossibly high value, of everything you take for granted."

—*The Stranger* (Seattle)

"Perhaps among a next wave of books about gay folks as full American citizens that doesn't bother walking them through schematic journeys meant to stand in for the American Gay Experience."

—*Salon*

"Sicha's uncanny, absurdist reduction is more than just a fun-to-read ruse: *Very Recent History* shames you, the reader, for losing sight, on a day-to-day basis, of just who is controlling your world. . . . [It] is exultant in a way no mere clever premise can be."

—NewYorker.com

"To portray gay life in the city as Sicha has done—in a manner that's both realistic and insightful—would be a noteworthy accomplishment in any era, but it must be considered particularly remarkable in today's publishing climate, in which major publishing houses offer readers more gay characters written by straight authors than by gay ones. Which is not to say you should read *Very Recent History* out of a sense of obligation or guilt; it's a beautifully written and carefully documented (and often very funny) book about a group of people that, to our society's collective detriment, continues to be largely ignored, dismissed, and stereotyped."

—*The Millions*

"Sicha's prose, sweet and alienating by turns, transforms a city I know well and a year I lived through into something odd and wonderful."

—Clay Shirky, author of *Here Comes Everybody*

"Sicha vivisects the student-loan crisis, finance capital, and other plagues in the arch tone of one explaining it all to a naïf from the future—a rhetorical device that trains a floodlight on the great hypocrisies of our time."

—*Elle*

"I love Choire Sicha's writing, which is as taut and tense as the neck of a Wall Street banker on the day of the world financial collapse of 2008. *Very Recent History* reads like a novel written by Hemingway, if he had given in to his gay tendencies and moved to New York. But it's actually a thinly veiled nonfiction account of New York in the time we live, in which nothing matters anymore—except maybe money—and everyone is disconnected, and how very sad and lonely this is, especially for our hero, who is anything but that. It's a true story of the quiet desperation that comes from a world full of meanness—and hype. It's also an intensely political book, quietly outraged at the overlords who are steadily making a once vibrant city fit for habitation only by the wealthy and privileged. *Very Recent History* takes on all the right things."

—Nancy Jo Sales, author of *The Bling Ring*

"The only book our ancestors will need to divine how accidentally these City people lived; how fecklessly they loved; how strangely they used their money; how deliberately they drank too much, worried, fooled around, hurt their friends, hurt themselves; and how they occasionally tried to outdo their fanatical self-interest and love somebody else. This book would start a revolution if we knew better."

— Rosecrans Baldwin, author of
Paris, I Love You But You're Bringing Me Down

VERY
RECENT
HISTORY

CHOIRE SICHA

VERY RECENT HISTORY

AN ENTIRELY FACTUAL ACCOUNT
OF A YEAR (C. AD 2009)
IN A LARGE CITY

HARPER ● PERENNIAL

NEW YORK ● LONDON ● TORONTO ● SYDNEY ● NEW DELHI ● AUCKLAND

HARPER PERENNIAL

A hardcover edition of this book was published in 2013 by
HarperCollins Publishers.

VERY RECENT HISTORY. Copyright © 2013 by Choire Sicha. All
rights reserved. Printed in the United States of America.
No part of this book may be used or reproduced in any
manner whatsoever without written permission except in
the case of brief quotations embodied in critical articles
and reviews. For information address HarperCollins
Publishers, 195 Broadway, New York, NY 10007.

HarperCollins books may be purchased for educational,
business, or sales promotional use. For information please
e-mail the Special Markets Department at SPsales@
harpercollins.com.

First Harper Perennial edition published 2014.

Designed by Fritz Metsch

Library of Congress Cataloging-in-Publication Data has
been applied for.

ISBN 978-0-06-191431-7 (pbk.)

14 15 16 17 18   OV/RRD   10 9 8 7 6 5 4 3 2 1

For David

In Russia, if you told two people they could both become richer, but one would become wealthier than the other, they would take the proposition, no problem. In New York, people surveyed rejected this scenario. Only in New York would people rather be poorer if they knew that, at the same time, someone else wasn't getting ahead either.

—W. MICHAEL COX,
former chief economist
at the Federal Reserve Bank of Dallas

No man has ever hung from the rafters of a second home.

—DAN BEJAR

n.b. Many names have been changed.

I.

There was, for a while, a very large and very famous city. For an even shorter while, the richest man in town was its mayor. This seemed, for the time that it was true, like a very improbable coincidence.

More than eight million three hundred thousand people lived in this city then, but, by any sane criteria, only a few hundred of those people mattered to any single one of the others. One or more sex partners. The woman behind the counter at the nearest deli. Colleagues and coworkers, if the person in question was employed. The friends acquired along the way, like white hairs on a black sweater, from compulsory public school or discretionary college. College was an advanced form of education that usually cost a lot of money and that, in general, at least two out of three young people started, but only one in two would finish. One grew up with these intense school friendships, and then, as one grew older, those friends were joined, or sometimes replaced, with new people: friends of former lovers, and lovers of current friends. A favorite bartender or waiter, maybe. A millionaire, probably, or one of the seventy-one billionaires that then called the City home.

Beyond that bright bubble was a hazy landscape of everyone else. From that middle distance came the potential of a perfect match, the perfect accident, the perfect path to money or renown. It milled in every bar or party or tedious elevator. A new person would snap into focus and color for a second before blurring off.

Each person lived and moved and worked in his own thin particular slice, like a glass plate in a high, compressed stack. The happier, richer people, it was imagined, were up above in ever-thinner, ever-shinier glass plates. People with all the freedom, or a great job, or a loving boyfriend, or at least an empty and gorgeous apartment.

And below: thick slabs of the poorer, the lonelier, and the hopelessly left behind. Those were people who'd gambled maybe with actual money and lost, or who had never had anything to begin with. There were so many more of them, an all-day warning to the foolishly ambitious or the reasonably aspirational.

From time to time, everyone could imagine himself near the top, climbing the face of this great glass pyramid, a feeling brought on by the fleeting exhilaration of a new job, or a great outfit, or an unexpected night of kissing in a doorway.

The Mayor, who employed at his private company at least ten thousand people, took an annual salary of only one dollar from the City while he held office. He leased seven hundred thousand square feet of business space in a building with his name on it, fifty-five stories tall. The building was completed just as he finished his first four-year term as mayor.

The tower was then only the fourteenth tallest building in the City. It was a slaty blue and everything around it was gray: gray gravel in the tucked-away driveway for all the drivers, gray stone curbs beneath the darker coats on the men who stood attentive at the slick glassy doors. This secret driveway gave a magical sense of the building being off the great sturdy grid of the City, which was all laid out in hard lines, except at some of the quiet and old edges, where the grid stuttered or became obscure, mired in its own history.

In addition to the Mayor's business offices this building had 105 apartments.

A hedge fund operator and investor named Peter Thiel lived there. A hedge fund took rich people's money—at their own request—and made more money with that money. In his apartment were floor-to-ceiling windows, with floor-to-ceiling curtains. Everything in it was gray and blue and black—a long dark table, with white linens, where his private chef made him light and delicious breakfasts when he was in town.

A very famous and very beautiful pop singer named Beyoncé owned an apartment there.

A TV anchor named Brian Williams lived there. His job was to uncover, or to at least read aloud, the news, which then came streaming into people's apartments, for the benefit of a company that was part-owned by General Electric. General Electric was at the time one of the world's most profitable companies. It was started by the man who first distributed electrical power just 120 years prior to this time.

Actually, both the current and a former chief of General Electric lived in the Mayor's building where Brian Williams and Beyoncé also lived.

Now nearly everyone in the City paid to have General Electric's news on the TV, and to have General Electric's power in their homes. They'd open up their refrigerators and the electric cold would seep out all around them.

When it was new, a 1,360-square-foot two-bedroom apartment—so, a not particularly large one—in that building was listed at 5.1 million dollars. A 1,726-square-foot two-bedroom apartment could be rented for 17,000 dollars each month—there were then twelve months in a year—which meant 204,000 annually.

One resident, Marc Dreier, a lawyer, had paid 10.4 million dollars for a four-bedroom apartment on the thirty-fourth floor. He couldn't live there any longer because he was now going to live in a prison, which was run by the government at that time. He was to stay there for twenty years; the laws he had broken included those prohibiting money laundering, and there were five counts of wire fraud and some other things, and so the apartment and everything in it was sold, to a man in the reinsurance industry named Ajit Jain, for just 8.2 million dollars.

"Reinsurance" was a kind of business transaction, where a company that sold insurance then transferred some of its insurance risk across multiple companies.

"Insurance" was an idea where, if you had something that you valued a lot, like an expensive painting or a child, you could pay a relatively small amount of money to a company and, if the painting was stolen or the child died, the company would pay you the agreed-upon value of the missing, or dead, object or person.

Companies offered this insurance because they made the payments just expensive enough that, almost always, the amount of money they were paid for these policies in total was more than they had to pay to replace people's paintings and children.

The "almost always" was what they called "the risk."

The contents of Marc Dreier's apartment that became Ajit Jain's apartment included a bottle of Laurent-Perrier Cuvée Rosé Brut, an alcoholic beverage that cost between 80 and 90 dollars. Also Ajit Jain found himself the owner of a fruit pie, kept cold in the refrigerator. A pie was a dessert made from flour and butter and, in this case, raspberries and peaches, but, unfortunately for its new owner, this one had already been half consumed.

ONE COLD NIGHT in winter a young man named John walked down a street in the City. It was free to walk on the streets, although to take a public conveyance, such as a subway or a bus, cost money.

"Hey, do you have a dollar?" said a man who did not have a home, and whose practice of employment was that he would ask passersby for money.

"Sorry," said John.

"It's okay, I can tell you're not rich," said the homeless man.

"That makes two of us," John said.

Before the winter had begun, a contagion had started in the City and swept across the country. A number of the City's companies—particularly the commercial and investment banks, and the insurance companies with whom they did business—had made some poor choices, and the effects of those choices had rippling economic consequences. Companies, hungry for cash, or at least

afraid of a lack of it, had begun to "lay off" employees—
terminating their employment agreements, which weren't
really much of agreements anyway since most of the
country had laws that treated employment as temporary.
That meant that employees could be fired for any or no
reason. At the same time, it was also always legal for employees to quit their jobs. In any event, companies needed
the cash because fewer people were consuming what they
made, or, just as likely, because they had been told by
their experts and advisers that soon fewer people would
consume what they made. Also, for sure, they wanted to
give more money to the people who ran the companies.
Two and a half million jobs had already disappeared. That
was a lot of money to save—or to pocket.

The City was a rich place—in a sense, the richest place
in the whole country—and so its economy, where the
contagion had started, was damaged but not devastated.
Still, it was a quiet panic. The people of the City, in the
aggregate, spent less money, but did not stop. Some expensive things dropped in value, like paintings, and well-
made clothes, and even apartments, somewhat, too. In
the rest of the country, many houses and apartments
became drastically less valuable, but that wasn't nearly
as true in the City. But what all this meant was that there
were many people without jobs, and many people afraid

of losing their jobs, and those who did have jobs often did not have much to do. What it really meant for the City was that the ability for many people to change jobs came to a near standstill for much of the year to come.

John worked, as did many people in the City, in the office of a corporate entity that was privately owned. Some companies were owned "publicly." This meant that, to one extent or another, individuals or companies could buy "shares"—little pieces—in the company and therefore become its owner, or one of its many owners. But the company at which John worked was controlled by a small group of people, and it was just between them and the entity that profit or loss flowed. Like many private smaller companies, this was just one of a suite of companies that had little to do with each other except being owned by the same person or family. Some of those companies were profitable—earning more than they spent. This one was not.

The walls of this office were painted a cheap white color and the carpets were a darker noncolor. A full-time employee, John was paid every two weeks by the corporation and received some small amount of vacation, and some amount of his health insurance cost was covered by his company's owner.

This office was a modified "open plan," meaning that

there were few interior partitions and few interior walls. The mayor of the City was a proponent of open plan office use, which he had installed both at his company and at the antique City Hall as well, as much as was possible there, creating a "bullpen" of a vast office. Other big corporations had done the same. At the banks and financial service firms in the City, lowly vice presidents sometimes sat next to managing directors—a title that conveyed more prominence, and greater financial rewards. The idea was to air out the secrets that happened behind closed doors, to allow for chance to create connections. Well, really, the original idea was to pack more people into smaller amounts of space, thereby saving money. The good stuff was just a side effect, as well as a handy sales pitch.

This open plan idea, like a bonfire or declaration of love, had to be executed completely or not at all. It didn't work to make an open plan for the lesser-paid workers while retaining private spaces for the more important managers. But for now, across the City, a great number of people sat at work, in rows or at tables, and the less important they were, the farther inside the building they were seated, which meant, mostly, being farther removed from any windows. So from the inside of the offices, it seemed like these workplaces were, at best, an endless shelving unit or, at worst, a livestock pen where the workers were kept like sheep and the managers, all around in their offices, were the shearers.

In John's case, his employer had built a bullpen for the staff, though it wasn't really a true bullpen, as the shallow desks had short little carpeted dividers that gave workers a small sense of privacy. Workers could pin things to these fake walls if they wanted. Then in the middle of the bull-pen was a double row of two desks that faced each other. So there was a hierarchy there too: the people who sat around the outside "U" of the room and faced the walls had more privacy, while the people who sat in the middle, like an "I" inserted into the "U," had less. And then there was a row of offices, at the open top of the "U" of the bull-pen, which blocked the only wall with windows.

The supervisory staff worked in those offices. The biggest and most private of the offices belonged to their boss, Thomas, a rather crazed steel-haired man in khakis, just old enough to be the father of the youngest of his employees. He was always loose with a riot of words and prone to extravagant monologues with endless and excruciating pauses. Everyone adored him. Thomas reported to the owner of the company, who was young—not much older than John. The owner was fairly new: He had bought this company recently—instead of having created it himself—to add to his other companies.

In the change in ownership, Thomas had expressed happiness publicly, but the rumors in the office held that he had been paid one million dollars to stay on running the company. Thomas and the owner did not particularly get along, although they said they did to anyone who asked.

This was a traditional disagreement: The owner wanted to spend less money, in order to be "profitable." Thomas wanted to spend more to do the same. In any event, the company's costs overran its revenue.

If a worker sat in the bullpen, sometimes he could see a door fly open and someone would say, "Can I see you in my office please?" Often this was friendly, someone just wanted to gossip or plot. Alliances of the workplace were divided along the physical outlines established in the office: employees with doors and the employees beyond them.

Most of the light in the office was provided by the cold baking of fluorescent strips overhead. Often the bullpen staff would leave those lights off and burn only a few incandescent lamps, and the room would become suddenly quite dark and cozy and pleasant. Then in the office one would feel like a young child in a library at the drab end of a winter's day.

ALMOST EVERYTHING IN the City was capital. The offices were to make money; the buildings were to make money; inside the buildings and the offices, people were employed to make things that made money. And then around these pillars were services: restaurants, bars, shops, cobblers, dressmakers, all to serve the people who were employed making money. So: almost everything. Everything except love, probably. People in the City didn't often make explicit matches of their children for the transfer of money or goods. But the arrangements of love had an old-fashioned lag to them, in which capital was attached. For instance, people talked about "marrying well," which meant that someone was marrying someone rich. For instance also, there were all the attendant issues of cohabitation. Of necessity or for simple matters of equality, there came the sharing, in some way, of money incoming and outgoing, and purchasing or not purchasing things, and paying for the electricity. There was also a custom of gift-giving at the time of the actual legal ceremony of marriage. When contracted, the parties would join in accepting gifts or, even more boldly, in dictating which gifts would be accepted. Many people made long lists of things they wanted to receive and everyone bought them and they were delivered. Frequently a wedding would be celebrated with a party of great expense. Hundreds of guests would be fed; spaces much larger than the traditional house were paid for; musicians were hired; people now came from far away, where once it was customary for only local people to celebrate a union. The arrangements often cost tens of thousands of dollars, if not hundreds of thousands of dollars, and it was frequent that the parents of those to be wed shared in this expense, as if the expense of this undertaking could not reasonably be assumed by the parties embarking on what was often referred to as a "new life."

This was a messy stew of old and new ideas. Marrying for love was a brand-new practice.

The customs of love in general had dictates, although there were many disagreements, many minority opinions. Early on, the rules concerned who should, or could, pay for things like the purchase of food in restaurants, and what that meant, this little gift-giving of things to be digested.

As the relationship developed, the pertinent matters became who would pay for the residence, who would make more money and how it would be shared. Love suffered most when issues of capital intruded. It bred distrust and bad feeling. In this way, the City and love were at odds.

Sometimes people would simply declare themselves married—even with no one there to observe this declaration. But declarations of marriage became more onerous and bureaucratic over time. To be truly married, an official had to preside over the declaration, and the couple involved had to pay a fee in order to be licensed by the government. So only the official could say who was wed and who was not.

The state became extremely busy deciding which domestic arrangements were legal and which were not. In this time with which we are concerned, there were some arrangements that society utterly forbid: it was illegal for people of a certain age to have sex with people under a certain age—these ages were picked to define "adult" and "child," but didn't always quite hit the mark—and it was illegal to force people to have sex. And there were some laws that were less sensible and were quickly falling out of favor. For instance, it was illegal to exchange money for sex, and it was illegal for men to marry men and women to marry women. It had also, until quite recently, been illegal for people of some different ancestries to marry. As well, it had been illegal for two people to have kinds of sex that couldn't result in the conception of another human being.

Sometimes the people prosecuted the crimes—or at least the criminals—themselves. Shame or violence was almost as good a punishment as imprisonment. But almost always, people were more forward-thinking than the laws. And the laws that fell out of favor, they didn't stay laws forever.

JOHN HAD GRADUATED from his professional school just four months prior to starting this job, which he had now held for a couple of years. He was very young and very thin, in the fashionable way of that time. He had freckles that would come and go in the summer sun, and reddish-brown hair: a handsome chipmunk. He was quick with words and he had no sense of smell and he couldn't drive a car and his eyes were pretty bad, so sometimes he wore these old glasses that made him look funny; they were blocky and dumpy and incongruously old. Often in the bullpen he'd put his face right up to his computer. He liked working, but he still remembered the freedom of that summer after graduation—everything had been so easy.

He had worked briefly as a nonemployee, a "freelancer," and that meant he made more money because so-called "freelance" pay was generally higher. It was expected that the freelancer would pay all his or her own benefits— like health insurance—and, at the conclusion of each year, taxes. Taxes were a percentage of everyone's earnings that paid for everything the government bought or built or wanted to maintain. And as well, he didn't have to be anywhere, didn't have to get up early and go into the office, any office, every day.

Except he'd also really messed up. Because that free-lance situation had been the first time he'd really worked, and because the taxes weren't taken out of his checks that summer as they were for full-time employees.

John had somehow reported only 3,669 dollars in income. The state had corrected this to 13,134 dollars in income. The government had said he owed something like 3,000 dollars.

When he started working full time, the company started setting aside the taxes for him, sending that portion of his income directly to the government. For most workers, the job would take out "too much," and so when people filed their taxes with the government, in a great wild flurry of forms and mathematics, people would then get a "refund." But John didn't get his "refunds," which would have been about 600 dollars each, because they went to pay off those old taxes.

Also the number that he owed kept going up because the government assessed "interest," as a "penalty."

He took home 2,200 dollars a month.

His expenses were 800 dollars for his half of the monthly rent—his cousin lived with him—and about 100 dollars for "utilities," which were the electrical power for the appliances and the lights and such, and water, and cable television. And then there were his debts. He didn't like to think about that. So after paying some of that, as much as he could face, he had about 900 or 1,000 dollars to spend each month, which was about 33 dollars a day. The subway to work every day took a little. Food took a little. Beers were 3 dollars. Every two weeks, he'd run out of money, and have just 20 or 40 dollars to last through Tuesday, Wednesday and Thursday.

SEX WAS A very unsatisfying practice at this time, considered animal and messy, and also dangerous. It had been dangerous for a long time, but now most nonlethal diseases were treatable, and also women could largely control whether they became pregnant. Pregnancy was the most lethal byproduct of sex. But there were still diseases that were not curable.

Sex itself was hard enough. Some people could achieve sexual satisfaction through only very specific means. For instance, dressing up in pirate hats, or as lions or puppies, or as corporate brands and characters. Some people couldn't achieve sexual climax without being punched in the stomach. Some people could achieve sexual intimacy with only one particular gender. Most people at this time believed there were two of those. And many believed these two genders were very distinct—almost separate species—and so they should have different roles in life. Many, though, found this ridiculous.

People made great and complicated arrangements to satisfy their urges.

But many people had less elaborate sexual structures—or "preferences"—so it was often easy, at least at first, for them to mate, or have sex, without even much of a thought to a prolonged commonality with a partner.

Sometimes people refused to acknowledge their sexual selves, leading to later trouble with mates. They hadn't been doing what they wanted, but they hadn't known it. For instance, many people wanted to have sex with a number of people, but they, by habit or by pressure, ended up in agreements that they would have sex with just one person only. But then their desires won out over their agreements.

Others, in various minorities of taste or persuasion, obsessed over their choices. If they were excited only by violence, or if they had to gaze upon pictures of, say, lesser mammals before sexual activity, they sometimes had to go to great lengths to solicit willing—if not even compatible—partners.

The arrival of the Internet—in its earliest, flattest state, of sending words, and then pictures, and then moving pictures—was most transformative of this endeavor, even more than it was for entertainment and the sale of retail products. The Internet, as people knew it then, was only about twenty years old, but most of the products and experiences on the Internet were even more recent than that.

Only through the early tentative arrival of full-world search could fellow enthusiasts of very particular sexual procedures easily identify each other.

And so could everyone else: people who wanted to meet to make children, people who wanted someone with whom to grow old, fellow adherents to a religion, people who were monogamists—or temporary monogamists.

But already, even though this was in the exciting early days of a virtual society, organic or accidental meeting in the real world—the face-to-face first blush and chemical systems rush—was seen as something prized, something original, something the flat Internet, even with all its growing reach and inclusion, couldn't offer.

JOHN'S FRIEND CHAD had a real office job and took home 425 dollars a week. This was a job that young people wanted. It opened doors; it introduced him to people, mentors maybe, famous people, intellectuals.

And then he quit. Chad realized that people didn't start

at the bottom and work their way up anymore. This was an outmoded idea. Instead of working at a desk all day, he started tutoring rich people's children, for money. He went to an agency that matched him with parents in the City. His rich clients were people who were essentially unaffected by any of the current anxieties about the economy, except attitudinally. They were supposed to be concerned, so they were. Or they pretended to be concerned. For instance, they would not go on an expensive vacation. These were people who all knew people who had suddenly gone broke. But it was like a mystery: Who would lose everything? Who was working at a financial firm, for instance, that would go bust?

Overall, the parents who hired Chad would probably spend five to ten thousand dollars for an increase in test scores of less than a hundred points on the all-important tests for college admission, which were called the SATs. They were paying Chad for one hundred minutes a week, to help their children focus. They could get the same result on their own from twenty dollars' worth of practice books. Or Chad could do two sessions, with practice questions, for ten times that amount, and the children would benefit just the same.

But for Chad it was a good thing that he had quit his job. He had more time to conduct his social life. Chad was cute, but he had been single for a while. He was trim and pale and had curly brown hair that grew wild, and deep brown eyes, usually obscured behind glasses that made him look like the sort of person with whom a rich person would entrust their children.

At a friend's urging, Chad made a profile on a dating website called DList. It was run by a guy named Daniel, a sort of well-known promoter of—among other things, like not-really-erotic erotic film festivals—sex parties. While some used the site in a goal-oriented way, Chad used it more or less socially. You would "go on" to the site and see who was "around," and you could "chat" with those people. It introduced the right levels of choice and randomness into a digital meeting place.

There were all these people on the site that Chad knew but didn't really know, like they were Internet friends of friends or he'd seen them "around." And then he searched in his neighborhood, and there was Diego's profile.

They both lived in a quiet corner of the City, far from the busy center. The City, long since graded and drained of most of its lakes and marshes, with its pretty houses high on its hills, was exposed to its wide, deep harbor. Down low at the harbor were its tall, cold buildings, where trade had always happened. Up between the two rivers the tall buildings fell away, then rose again, and then once again fell, as wildness and hills and cliffs surrounded the waterways that pushed south past the City. Each day the harbor and its briny water pushed up the rivers, and each day the clean rivers flushed down. Ports first abounded on all sides, until most of the ports were replaced by highways. Aside from the central column of the City the houses shrank in their tight rows and neighborhoods ambled. There were little hills with the grander homes of the rich. And there were little swamps and gullies, with the warehouses and the houses of the poor. Chad and Diego lived in a flat stretch of neighborhood that was just right.

Diego was this brown-eyed, brown-haired man, with pale skin and tough almond eyes. Chad liked what Diego wrote about himself, and so he chatted him on the website. Diego worked and was in school at night. He would have been graduating in May if he didn't also have a full-time job. But he thought this was good because it wasn't like there were any jobs anyway.

They chatted for about thirty or forty minutes.

Chad typed, Why don't we talk on the phone?

WHEN JOHN LEFT his undergraduate college with his degree, a professor wrote him a four-page letter of introduction to the world. He could use this for his application to professional school, or to gain entrance to places of employment. It included some lines about John's personal life: "John's mother died of breast cancer when he was five. His father subsequently died of a stroke. The family's financial situation had been badly eroded by medical bills and nothing was left."

John's oldest brother was fourteen years older, thirty-nine, and already had two boys, John's nephews. Then there was the next brother, who was thirty-five, ten years older, and was about to get married. He'd always hated that John was born, John thought. They had fought a lot growing up, but because of this, or in spite of this, they had a good amount of mutual respect for each other in their adulthoods.

Sometimes, when John and Chad were out, John listened to Chad talk with his own brothers on the phone and was mystified by the affectionate way they spoke to each other. John had never said "I love you" to his oldest brother, and the only time his brother ever said "I love you" to John was right after their dad had his stroke and John was in the house and his brother came to pick him up to take him to the hospital.

"I've never told you this, but I love you," his brother said.

"Don't get carried away," John said.

MOST PEOPLE AT this time ate meat. The opinion regard-ing the treatment of animals by humans, in order of what was considered most evil to most unremarkable, went: the ivory trade, which was the slaughter of elephants in a distant land for their tusks; animal medical experimen-tation; the skinning and wearing of fur; industrial meat farming; meat eating; dairy farms; petting zoos; zoos; the eating of eggs; the drinking of milk; the keeping of household pets.

CHAD AND DIEGO agreed that the written self, the online persona, was too difficult and queasy a form to really gauge a person and so decided to move quickly from the online to the real world. How can you know if you like a person just based on what they tell you, not what you see? Not that seeing wasn't its own problem. Chad loved putting on a persona, but for understanding who to date, how could you tell online? Like you could be funny as an online persona and then be anxious or unfunny or just slow in person.

On one Sunday night, they talked on the phone for several hours. Diego was avoiding studying for school. They discov-ered that Diego had worked with Chad's roommate once upon a time. Other than that, Chad and Diego had little real-world overlap. So Diego picked up Chad after work and they went for a burger and then to a dance performance and

Diego came over to Chad's house afterward and together they rode the subway to work in the morning.

JOHN THOUGHT THAT people came to the City, and only then did they realize just how very many people there were. They arrived casually, just to try it out, to see what happened, but wound up getting caught in the great impossible sea of people: With so many, how could you choose one deserving of all your attention? With so many choices, you could easily think that there was always another better one.

The friends who accompanied John to the City—his first real boyfriend, Jordan, and his best pal, Ralph—were like a diary. Friends were imprinted with the permanent record. Ralph, for instance, remembered the day at college when John had, with great excitement, shown him a picture of Jordan.

When John and Jordan broke up, John was promptly devastated and then almost as immediately intrigued by all the chances there in the City to see all these people who were more exciting, more handsome, more whatever. But none of them stuck, none made one percent of the impact that Jordan had made. Ralph knew how John had decided, after Jordan, that he'd never be in love again, that he'd never find anyone who'd stick.

Ralph had been fairly religious in college, quite strait-laced. But by the time he and John went off to the same graduate school, they went out six nights a week, to the City's bars and clubs. Ralph was tall too, and thin, and gorgeous. They didn't always go out together because their interests overlapped in only some ways. Ralph felt like he had three different identities that he exercised on different days and in different neighborhoods of the City, small slices of life often invisible to outsiders.

And so they'd go out separately or together, and get home at three a.m., and then go to class, then study all evening, then go out all night again.

Then they all got jobs and eventually Ralph was going out only once a week, or once every two weeks.

And then John and Ralph saw less and less of each other, because Ralph had started seeing someone for a while, until it ended in heartbreak and Ralph left the country for a while. Now John could watch Jordan with his new lover, Jeff. They had a good thing going, John thought, and with the time and distance, he could appreciate what they had together. They'd never cheated; they'd settled on each other exclusively. Well, actually, Jordan had cheated on Jeff in the first six months, once. But then, for years, never again. That was pretty good. That kind of thing seemed impossibly rare.

John thought about how a writer had described babies learning words as though they were a continual series of floating spoons. A baby just grabs onto one here and grabs onto another there, and that's how John thought about boys right now. Like they're all hanging out, out there in space but in reach, and John could just close his eyes and pretty much grab any one of them.

LOTS OF PEOPLE—most people—wanted a TV in their apartment. A TV was a thin device for displaying broadcasts sent by corporations. People paid for the TVs just once, and then, like electricity, paid each month for what came to the TV. Even though you paid for the TV programming, big companies also paid to show off their products on the TV, so the companies that distributed the TV programming made money two ways. Some people had cars, and some of those people had TVs in their cars. The elevators that went up the tall buildings had TVs. Taxicabs, the cars with drivers for hire in the City, had TVs, but they weren't really real TVs; you couldn't choose what to watch, but at least you could choose to turn them off.

THE OWNER OF John's company threw a party to celebrate his company at the Four Seasons, which was considered one of the City's most sophisticated restaurants. This was what people with a lot of money did: throw expensive parties to draw attention to themselves.

The place was magnificent. "The walls are hung with a fortune in art and tapestries by such modern geniuses as Picasso, Joan Miró, and Jackson Pollock," wrote a reviewer for what was then the City's chief newspaper, fifty years earlier. That writer would go on to win a charity auction in which the prize was a limitless-price dinner at a restaurant of his choice; he paid 300 dollars—about 1,200 dollars, adjusted for "inflation"—for this prize. He chose a restaurant called Chez Denis—in a different country even!—and the bill, for two, came to 4,000 dollars. When adjusted for inflation to this time, that was a bit shy of 16,000 dollars. At the time, everyone was outraged.

But many people spent that amount of money on a single dress, or a wedding party, or a very inexpensive car, or a month's rent, if you lived in the building with the Mayor's name on it.

The state's brand-new governor came and spoke at this party. The president of John's professional school came. At this party, in fact, John saw most of the very rich people that controlled the various institutions of his life. The new governor was not particularly rich, and would not be the governor for long. The previous governor, though, was nearly as rich as the Mayor. Despite the fact that they occupied the same rarified tier of wealth, they weren't really friends, though they claimed to be. But then, a large amount of money was often isolating.

The ex-governor's father had more than 500 million dollars, though he himself had grown up very poor. He gave the ex-governor, his son, a very nice apartment at 985 Fifth Avenue. His father, in fact, had caused the building to be built. The family took in more than a million dollars a year in rents paid by other people.

Because his father was rich, the governor grew up with other rich people; he went to a private high school—that is, he received the mandatory education for young people, but he took it at a school that you paid to attend, because it was a much better school—and then to expensive colleges and professional schools.

But for one summer while he was at school, he gave it all up. He went about to rural places in the country, picking vegetables and doing construction. He wanted to find out what the country was like for normal people. This experience convinced him that, even if one didn't have a college degree or, say, a college degree from a not-very-good school, one could "make it" in the country—provided one wanted to work really hard. This was not a terribly original idea. In fact, it was an idea so popular that to object to it was considered intellectually treasonous.

At long last, he'd grown up and been in charge of the whole state. But then he had to leave his job governing: He had paid women other than his wife to have sex with him. More important, he had lied about it. Everyone in the City was very upset about that, though some were more amused than scandalized.

The new governor had to announce his infidelities as well, but he had never lied or broken any laws, so he was welcome at the Four Seasons.

The Mayor came to this party as well. The owner of John's company was nowhere near as rich as the Mayor, but he was, obviously, rich as well, because his father was rich.

The people there were in charge of the actual landscape of the City. That meant that they controlled the dirt, the stones, the buildings, the tunnels, the sightlines, the scene, and, less so but not much less so, the movements of the people within the landscape.

The physical landscape was a harder and harder thing to control. Though always malleable, foot by foot, the City had become more calcified as it grew up over the decades. For one thing, fewer grand disasters happened.

For instance, on one incredibly cold night about 175 years before this time, 674 buildings—all of them south of Wall Street—burned down in a single fire.

Unfortunately, many insurance claims weren't paid to the owners of those buildings, because some of the insurance companies burned down, ending their operations.

Those charred acres were an opportunity. All sorts of physical landscape was claimed and made and shaped.

Still later in the City's life, whole neighborhoods were bulldozed and claimed, even when they hadn't burned down.

But that sort of thing didn't happen much anymore.

Although, to be fair, in the Mayor's two terms, nearly one-fifth of the land in the entire City had been rezoned. "Rezoning" was what it was called when you changed the designation of a block or a neighborhood, allowing owners to build more—almost never less—usable space on a particular piece of property. Rezoning was a gift to the owners of property. You did some studies and had some meetings, or sometimes not even that, and the City declared that this block—where it had previously been ordered that, say, only low industrial buildings could be built—could now accommodate tall residential buildings. And then someone came along—or, more likely, was waiting in the wings—and they borrowed a lot of money and they built the buildings, and sometimes didn't go broke along the way.

THE IDEA OF a distinct unit of money was, at that time, a little more than 5,000 years old, as near as could be told. The idea of precious metals being used as currency was maybe about 2,500 years old. The idea of a piece of paper standing in for a set value was almost exactly 1,000 years old.

So for a long time, money had been an object that promised a value, such as a piece of paper that said, with words, that it conveyed a certain amount. Prior to that, instead, money was a thing that actually had an independent value, such as gold or silver, which were chemical elements that were found in the ground.

Some people had, however, been using other things to stand in for value three thousand years ago. Sometimes people who used, say, shells as money made their arrangements quite sensibly, so that the larger or perhaps more rare the shell, the more the shell was worth. The shells could be so big that they were difficult to carry.

Shells, of course, could be found just lying here and there, and also they were replenished by living organisms. Gold and silver were not potentially limitless. There was only so much gold. In just a few years prior to this time, the largest amount of gold per year ever, in the history of humanity, had been taken out of the ground. Almost all through the rest of that decade, there was less and less gold found each year.

The gold was always deeper in the ground—"older" gold. Very little fresh gold was arriving from space. Only a small fraction of a percent of the gold had arrived from space recently, meaning, give or take, in the last four billion years.

Miners—working on behalf of corporations, not for themselves—took just a bit less than twice as much gold from the ground as they had some thirty years ago, and they found four times as much as they had ninety years ago. They wanted it all.

Not everyone was entirely in the system of money. The corporations were; they sold this gold on the markets in exchange for money. The miners were, for the most part, paid in money for retrieving the gold. But some people made their own systems of money. People in prisons, for instance, had no money or extremely little money, so they organized among themselves a system where their "money" had an actual value—which arose according to its scarcity. For one currency, some used cigarettes. For another, canned fish.

It seemed, over a period of many centuries, every group

of people large or small that organized a society invented a currency.

Where there was money, some would hoard it. Some would never get much of it. Some who had much of it would use it to get more. This was a sensible reaction to there being money.

Those who had very much money, who retained these markers of value, even if the value was very abstracted, could avail themselves of other people's money. They used their money as an insurance of the borrowed monies' return. This sort of money might not even be in paper form but might instead just be distributed through banks, whose job it was to hold money, and therefore the "actual" money might be put to thousands of different purposes by those banks and only be registered as attached to the current "owner" of the money by means of records.

Each person's money was like an excited band of pigeons that swooped and swooped and always, eventually, homed.

The government had chosen to, or was allowed to, retain the monopoly for creating the official money for the whole country. And then the government let the businesses decide how much the money was worth, although they influenced that value strongly. This idea went terribly wrong, around the world, from time to time—such as when governments would collapse, or would be forced into printing more paper that represented value without taking into account, or sometimes purposely ignoring, the thing from which that paper drew its value.

To be fair, the shell system wasn't much better. The obvious nonsecret to using shells as an economic marker is to become a better scavenger of shells.

The country once had a coin made of gold that represented its money, even while it had its own paper currency. But then, not long after, the government forbade its citizens from having very much gold. They were allowed shells, however, but the shells didn't get you anything, unless you were a shell collector and wanted to trade shells just for other shells or for, of course, money.

JOHN WENT OUT to Metropolitan, his favorite cozy little bar, particularly in the cold months. John met this guy, this great-looking guy, and they spent the night together. It was a crazy, energizing emotional experience, that thrill you get when you meet someone great and appealing, a kind of magic that was rare.

And apparently the guy really liked John too, because John read about it on the Internet on the guy's personal diary the next day: "Met this amazing guy last night," that sort of thing, and then it went into more really quite personal detail.

The thing is, John had been reading this guy's writing online for months—but when they met, he didn't connect the person to the persona. He actually read this stuff because he liked to make fun of it. The guy had not only a boyfriend but also an unending series of sex partners, sometimes for cash as well. He had amazing stories too. Sometimes John and his friends would read these stories together out loud. And then suddenly, the shock of intruding unexpectedly into this narrative, guest-starring in this Internet tale, was sort of like—what was it even like, having your activities of the night before published, with your name, in public? A little like opening the newspaper and reading a long and overwrought review of your own private diary, as recounted by someone who doesn't know at all the most important things there are to know about you.

Later on, the guy wrote about how upset and mystified he was that he never heard from John again.

THE MAYOR HAD not always been the mayor. There had in fact been many before him. He was the 108th. Early on in the life of the City, mayors were appointed, first by a regional governor, then by various elected councils of the City. Eventually—after a bit more than two hundred years—it was decided that people in general, the people who lived in the City, should decide which of them should be the mayor. There had been only forty-eight of these mayors that were elected. They were not all rich men in recent decades. The earlier appointed ones had tended toward wealthy backgrounds, naturally, because the people who were doing the appointing were wealthy and that's who they knew, but the elected ones were not all born rich or even made rich. One was an Irish immigrant turned police officer; some were lawyers and judges; a few were farmers; many were merchants; one was a locomotive engineer; at least a few were, or became while in office, crooks. The exposure to so much money was too much for them. Because people didn't live so long, only the last three previous mayors were still alive.

The Mayor was not allowed to be mayor anymore. Mayors weren't allowed to serve their four-year terms more than twice in a row. The people of the City had voted on it, two times, and a majority of them had voted in favor of this limitation. The immediately previous mayor had tried to extend his term by just three months, and this proposal had been roundly rejected.

CHAD LEFT TOWN, and Diego emailed with some fun advice for what to do overseas. Chad didn't want to be too much in contact with Diego too soon, so the email made him slightly nervous. He figured they'd talk when he returned. But then Chad found a poster glued to a wall that he knew Diego would like and he tried to tear it off to bring it back. Anyway it was impossible not to reply and soon they were emailing back and forth.

Then Chad got back to town and called Diego right away.

Soon enough, Diego asked Chad if he wanted to exclusively date each other. And after that emotional monogamy talk, they had a sexual monogamy talk. They decided they would sleep only with each other. The monogamy talk was precipitated by a question: How okay was it to be on sex-related websites, such as the one on which they had first become acquainted? So they talked about: Are you using this website for a social life? For a fantasy life? For meeting others? And which and what of those are okay? Because those online relationships can flip so quickly into reality, much as theirs had.

What had happened was that Chad had been checking his email on Diego's computer, and while on it, he found traces of Diego's visits to these sorts of sites on the public Internet. Diego said the Internet served a purpose both social and fantastic. The social aspect could extend to photos and interactions with real people—but the fantasy aspect was delimited by his online profile, which declared information about himself and his interests and clearly explained that he was in a relationship and not looking for "real-world" interactions. Chad understood the impulse but wasn't comfortable. Diego said that there had been no exceptions to their monogamy.

About a month into their relationship, Diego got tested for diseases. Chad had been tested just previous to that. And Diego had the tests run again, because they felt the relationship was getting serious, and then they stopped using condoms for sex. Condoms were what people had used for hundreds and hundreds of years to prevent themselves from giving other people diseases, or from getting those diseases, or to prevent pregnancy, whichever combination was applicable. Chad knew a lot of people who didn't even know what diseases they might have, and he couldn't understand that. The anxiety this gave him! Chad was a mild hypochondriac and at the same time was definitely reasonably afraid of dying and death. Two of Diego's best friends from public high school had a virus that jeopardized their health, and so the possibility of unexpected consequences was not abstract to him. He didn't need to be a hypochondriac to take his health seriously.

Diego had moved to their cozy isolated corner of the City not long ago, far from the skyscrapers, and had no friends there at all. Having Chad in the neighborhood made it now seem comfortable and private, instead of scary and new.

Diego's last boyfriend, of a year and a half, had just disliked Diego's friends. He said that he thought Diego's friends were too "pedestrian." So people were hesitant to meet Chad, because they felt so burned by the last boyfriend. Chad had the same thing—his last boyfriend had been very moody and self-absorbed. He didn't want to go out with Chad's friends, and when he was dragged out, he was just unpleasant.

Both of them, they thought, had learned from these experiences.

JOHN HAD MET Kevin, his other good friend, at a local bar called Eastern Bloc, back around the time that John had started his job.

John had been out with someone who'd gone to school with Kevin. John was not enjoying himself at all on this date, so he glommed onto Kevin. He thought Kevin was cute—Kevin was slightly redheaded, and the friendliest guy, with twinkly light eyes, clear skin and an incredibly symmetrical face. He had an attitude of being always game for anything. So instead of going home with his date, John went home with Kevin—and Kevin's boyfriend, Hassan.

Hassan was sort of the opposite in appearance of Kevin: He always looked stern or sly, with his dark hair and heavy eyebrows. They'd been together since college. But Kevin's boyfriend wasn't that interested and went to sleep on the couch, while Kevin and John kept the bedroom.

About a month later they contacted each other on Facebook; Kevin sent John a message. Facebook at this time was a worldwide social engagement system, nearly indistinguishable from the Internet itself. It seemed to Kevin that they both had an opening for a new friend. Kevin had a lot of friends from high school who'd all scattered, and he didn't have a best friend in the City. So they went straight from not knowing each other to hanging out four times a week. And they slept together sometimes but not for that long.

Kevin now worked part time—"freelance"—for a company that was owned by the cousin of the owner of John's company. Both these owners even had the same last name. Also, these two owners hated each other and never spoke. John's owner was probably richer than Kevin's owner, but only they would know about that for sure.

Before this new job, Kevin had gotten laid off from what had been only his second job since school. Lots of employers tended to get rid of more recent hires, although others tended to get rid of people who'd worked there the longest, as they were generally paid more. In this case, they fired half the office.

This is how they fired everyone.

Late in the week, at six p.m., the managers said that there needed to be a big office meeting. The office was also a big open room, just like the Mayor's office and John's office. In that room, the managers announced to the whole office that the firm was out of money and they needed to fire people.

But we're not going to tell you now who's fired, they said. Go home and we'll send you an email. And then, whenever you want to, you can come in and clean out your stuff.

So Kevin left and went to the gym, which was a "club" you could join for money and exercise, and there he ran on the treadmill. Then he got home and the email was waiting for him. He thought it was pretty outrageous, but while it was frightening, that such instability could be visited upon him out of the blue, he didn't feel shattered.

He had a friend, an older person who had gone to his same college, who had introduced him to the cousin of the owner of John's company. This new situation was fine! He was also getting "unemployment insurance" payments from the state, in addition to the money from this new job. All told, he was actually making more money than he

had before. He was seeing, like Chad, that being tradition-
ally employed was not a particularly worthwhile thing.

Kevin even had a savings account. He'd never borrowed
money—except for college, and he thought he would
be paying for that for the rest of his life. It was only 150
dollars a month right now—the first year he was out of
school, it was just 70 dollars; then they ratcheted it up a
little. Soon he was afraid it'd be 400 dollars a month, and
what then? But he had felt really informed about the responsibility he was taking on when he signed up: His parents also had school loans that they were still paying off.

After Kevin had graduated from school, he spent the
first year at his mom's house, in a northern suburb of the
City. He hadn't wanted to move straight from his mom's
into a house with his boyfriend, and so he got an apartment with a roommate, a wild foreign lady with multiple
cats, who talked to a psychic online all the time. But she
worked in the evenings and he worked in the day, so that
was okay, except, still, it was weird, so he finally gave in
and moved in with his boyfriend.

JOHN'S LANDLORD, A woman named Zofia, had a
400,000-dollar mortgage on his building. It had been in
her possession for about ten years. The cost of the building was 311,000 dollars, and presumably she used the rest
for improvements.

Each unit in the building—there were seven, including the ground floor—cost 1,400 dollars each month when she bought it, but then the rent prices were raised to 1,600 dollars each month.

That meant that the landlord had made 117,600 dollars in total each year from just that building. With the rent increase, she was making 134,400 dollars each year. She owned quite a few other things as well, many nearby, as was common. To own one thing was a sign that one could own other things like it.

The neighborhood was industrial near the edges, with four-story apartment buildings and retail storefronts off of a grimy main thoroughfare. It was a place that had long ago been poisoned by industry. But it was on a river, if you walked down that way, and you could see the skyscrapers just across the water. The very first house in the neighborhood had been built 350 years before, about eight blocks from where John lived, and all the land had been that house's farm. Now there were a bit more than 16,000 households living on what had been that one homestead. And the site of that first house was now just a small triangular intersection of streets and one tree.

Someone at some point had cut up and divided John's building, which was common practice. There was no telling what these buildings had been like originally, now made and chopped into little apartments.

Now John's own little apartment, half of the fourth floor, had a combined kitchen and living room, which had no windows. It was big enough for a little table and a cooking area and a small couch that faced a small television, which also directly faced a little bathroom off the living room. There were two bedrooms off the opposite side of this main room; those both had windows, and were big enough for a bed and a desk and a chair.

John's cousin lived in the other bedroom, and sometimes his girlfriend, who also had her own place. The apartment was, by the standards of most places and times, fairly terrible. Even the paint felt wrong; the windows were ill-fitting; the fixtures were ugly. John loved everything about it, he loved being home, and he never wanted to leave.

There was a desk, but it was covered in things, so mostly he worked in his little broken, sunken-in bed, surrounded by clothes and trash. The desk had one leg bent precariously in and a drawer with no handle. It was nearly impossible to open. That is where he put all the mail and bills from the year, on top of the bills from last year.

It was like a little nest.

He had this old white laptop computer, five pounds of keyboard and a screen. Mostly he used this for the Internet. It made crunching noises and wheezes. It was like one of the popular toys for children, made by a conglomerate called Fisher-Price. They made candy-colored blown-up nonworking versions of real-world things, like fake ovens. They were supposed to be instructional: things that made a game out of things like answering phones and being a doctor and performing light construction. Except John's computer was a dirty white, so it was like the spooky ghost of a Fisher-Price toy.

CHAD AND DIEGO never fought. They'd never actually, to date, had a fight that they'd call, in hindsight, a fight. They'd never even really snapped at each other.

The worst thing Diego had ever done was to be late to Chad's birthday dinner. The second-worst thing he'd ever done was, on their first date, he'd made fun of Chad in front of some people, but he'd been trying to make a joke, and it just came out wrong.

The worst thing Chad had ever done was that he insulted Diego's religion. He said something like, "Well, you're not really a Jew." While Chad had grown up Jewish, Diego hadn't.

"I'm funny all the time though, right, Diego?" Chad said to him in front of some people.

"Right," Diego said.

They slept together four nights a week or so, and they'd been together then for ten months. Chad was looking vaguely at professional schools, in different cities. Diego wasn't averse to maybe leaving the City after he finished school. And they both wanted to have kids someday. Or dogs. Or dogs and kids. Chad's mom had been twenty-five when she'd had him. He really liked having young parents. She was now fifty. So when he thought about having children, he thought about doing it sooner. His aunt had just had a child at forty, and he wasn't sure he knew what he thought about that.

Even though they were both so respectful and kind to each other, John never gave them much of a chance. The relationship, John thought, was too warm but never hot enough. Chad, he thought as well, was too young. And Diego was too freshly reformed from being out on the town: gone from being a boy who liked the bars and staying out late to being in school and at home with Chad. The reform was, like, spray-painted on, he thought. And John thought Chad was suspicious of Diego. And there were little things. Like, one night Chad got really drunk and said to John and all their friends, "You haven't had a chance to really see me single yet."

THEY WERE DRUNK.

"All these women! There's a lot of women in this bar," John said.

"I can't believe we've been ghettoized," said Chad.

"The looks. The claws coming out of eyes," said John.

"I don't want to hear it," Chad said.

JOHN AND HASSAN had a little bit of friction. Hassan was a very quiet person. John's loud and outgoing nature didn't always agree with him. So instead of having John over, Kevin would always go meet him out.

Kevin also thought maybe he would go to a professional school. All his ideas about where he saw himself in three years were vague. He had thought that by now he'd know.

Kevin and John were the most broke of all their friends, so sometimes Kevin would bring a six-pack of beer over to John's and they'd hang out inside, smoking cigarettes out the window.

Kevin and Hassan's relationship was hard to describe in terms of intimacy. They were very affectionate but increasingly less sexual. Sometimes Kevin got nostalgic for when they had sex all the time. But they'd been together since they were nineteen. There weren't exactly rules about what they could and couldn't do with other people; it was more like a principle: Respect the relationship, don't have torrid affairs. It was a fine line to straddle. Should they be allowed to sleep with someone more than once? It seemed strange to enforce that you could sleep with someone else only once. Why would that be more healthy? Wouldn't that just force you to have dreary, non-intimate secondary relationships?

Eventually Hassan thought that Kevin and John were a little too close. He thought: You talk online all day, you see each other all night and you're out till three in the morning, and you do it again the next day? Kevin found it hard to say no to John. John was persuasive to the point of bullying. Kevin had to learn how to say no to him. And John's reaction to that was, Why are you being so anti-social? And Kevin would say, I just need some time to be home and not be out. So Kevin was barely even going out on weekends now, much less weeknights. And Kevin's cats and boyfriend were happier about this too, and Kevin thought he probably was as well.

AROUND THIS TIME John had a recurring dream that he was at a dinner with all his friends and their lovers and he was the only one there who was all alone in the world.

A LETTER ARRIVED from Jason Hudson, DDS, and Ash M. Estafan, DDS, dated March 13. "DDS" stood for Doctor of Dental Surgery. It was a bill, and the amount owed was 447.64 dollars. The letter noted that payment was more than six months past due.

Leaving a bar late one night, a little drunk, John had simply fallen down on the street and cracked his two front teeth. The dentists had seen to him right away—they were the dentists of his boss, who had made the introduction—and they'd installed two temporary "crowns" on his teeth. They sat in his mouth and felt foreign.

These cappings could not be confused with "grills," removable gold and diamond-encrusted casings placed over the front teeth for the purpose of displaying wealth, a recent fad. John's, instead, were white. They were intended to look like real teeth, and they pretty much did.

John never paid and never returned. After more than a year of wear, his temporary crowns were thinning and turning, very slowly, to a translucent gray-brown.

IN THE MIDDLE of March, it was less terrible and biting out, and John went and bought a pair of tough denim trousers called jeans. Often riveted at stress points, jeans had originally been worn strictly for labor. They had since grown popular for daily wear, and even, sometimes, in less formal workplaces. There were now all kinds of jeans, from ones that cost fifteen dollars to ones that cost more than eight hundred dollars and came with gold-plated buttons even. John had been wearing a pair of jeans for over a year that had a big hole that split farther and farther down the front so that more leg was exposed each time he wore them.

And then Kevin called him, on Friday, at the end of the workday. "There's a sale for the next two hours at Uniqlo," he said. That was the name of a trendy but very inexpensive store that had recently arrived in the City. "Two jeans for fifty dollars."

So John left work and ran over and got two, one pair more professionally dark and trim, in a size 31, and one less dark and more skinny, in a size 32, which made him feel that he had gotten very large. He'd never worn a 32 before. His friends had told him to get ready for these sorts of moments, these signs of the body's transformation into manhood.

After that, he had a brief and loud dinner with all his family—his brothers, the sister-in-law, and their cousins—before the real plans for the night. He went over to a friend's house. Kevin and Hassan were there, and they sat around watching videos of a popular entertainer named Britney Spears on the Internet on the computer. These were videos that let you hear what her real voice was like when she was singing in concert, without the prerecorded backing tracks that made her sound like a good singer. They were all laughing, and they were thinking they'd just stay in and do this all night.

Then Chad and some friend of Chad's came over. Chad was in a terrible mood.

"Are you drunk right now?" Chad said to John.

"I dunno, a little, maybe," John said.

"What did you do before?" Chad asked.

"Oh, it was just a family dinner," John said.

"Right, you were probably the most drunk there, right?" Chad said.

"No, I was actually the least drunk out of everybody," John said.

"The least drunk of your family? Now that's depressing," Chad said.

Chad said something to Kevin that John didn't hear.

What? John asked later. "I can't even repeat it," Kevin said. "It's just so ridiculous that, like, I don't want to think about it anymore. I can't even say the words to you."

Everyone was having fun but Chad.

"Can we leave please?" Chad asked everyone. "I want to go somewhere. Can we go out? I want to go out please."

THERE WAS SOMETHING missing and no one quite knew what it was. This was an absence that people didn't really think about very much, or at all.

This was about fifty years since people began to understand how a virus "lived" and "ate" and "reproduced," and a hundred years since even the existence of a virus had become even remotely understood. So the first of the documented lentivirus plagues—the so-called "slow" viruses—took people by surprise. It took a while for people to catch on; these viruses were more than seven million, or so, years old.

The City was a big place, so two thousand deaths right away was not much to notice. The total number of deaths was ten times that five years later.

The number of dead had doubled three years later, and by then, there were estimated to be ten million people alive with this virus around the world. Once again the number of deaths in the City doubled within eight years. Around the country, more than half a million people died.

The winter that Chad and Diego met, there were only about a hundred thousand people with this virus in the City—almost exactly the same as the number of City residents who had died so far. A bit more than two-thirds of those dead people were men, which was because at least a full third and at most, and more likely, two-thirds of all those people were men who exclusively or at least sometimes slept with other men.

So we know from these numbers that some people were missing.

Say three hundred thousand men, minimum, disappeared—nearly all at once, in the long view—in the country.

Say at least fifty thousand men disappeared from the City over the course of John's life.

These were people who would have been coworkers, mentors, bosses, owners, millionaires, subway workers, neighbors, guys to pick up at bars, people at libraries, people on the Internet, people with advice, good or bad, or ideas, good or bad, or entrepreneurs, or adoptive parents, or stalkers on the Internet, or politicians, or knowing secretaries, or painters, or people in the next cubicle. But they weren't there.

JOHN WENT OVER to Amelia's house, just down the road from him, in his new jeans. Amelia was a moody, underpaid, waifish blonde from work. They got really stoned on marijuana. They were reading the Bergdorf Goodman catalogue, which was like a magazine but contained clothes and shoes and jewelry for people to come and buy at the store of the same name in the City.

"This is really good writing," John said, and he read some of it to her.

"That sounds beautiful," Amelia said.

After a while he realized that he was so stoned that he

had to leave, and so he went home, where his cousin and his cousin's girlfriend were watching a movie called *Shakespeare in Love*. John came in during the middle of a scene in which Shakespeare was writing one of his famous plays, and John couldn't stop screaming at the TV, so they told him to go to his room.

He turned on his personal computer and signed on to a website called Manhunt, a rather more transactional version of DList.

He was chatting with some guy whose screen name—his "handle"—was Ritalin. He had, John thought, a very attractive body. And yet John did not find his face as attractive. This guy was twenty-seven or twenty-eight, and John thought that he could start to see this aging in his face. The way that fat starts to pool beneath the chin, the way the skin around the eyes starts to sag, the way fat pulls away from the lines around the mouth revealing the skeleton beneath. He was nearing a cliff, though he hadn't gone over it yet. The hairline—it was just so slightly inching back. Almost receding but not.

"We should get drunk sometime soon," the guy wrote to John.

"Hell yes, we should," John wrote.

They exchanged real names. John searched the Internet. The guy was an actor, or wanted to be. He was 5'11" and weighed 135 pounds. He had 875 pictures, many of them of himself, on his Facebook page.

AT WORK, JOHN'S friend Sally smoked cigarettes, and his manager Timothy smoked cigarettes. Some other people did too, but not as frequently as they did. Cigarettes were made up of tobacco, a nightshade, and a secret cocktail of chemicals. They weren't allowed to smoke in the office though. That had been outlawed just twenty years before. They smoked on the street outside. You couldn't smoke inside anywhere. People once smoked while inside airplanes. Airplanes were like long air cars that flew fast in the sky, and you could buy a seat on one to travel to other cities and countries or, if you were really outlandishly rich, you could buy your own airplane. The planes gave off smoke too. At this time, everyone was still allowed to smoke in rental apartments, but quite soon they would not be allowed to smoke in parks or on beaches in the City. This was a way in which the Mayor was controlling behavior that was considered harmful. Cigarettes could kill you.

Smoking was a vice. Some of the other vices were alcohol, drugs, and, depending on who you asked, lying and cheating and cruelty.

So they would all traipse downstairs. They'd walk past

their boss's office. "Hey, kid!" Thomas would say to John.

It was a problem: One person would walk by another's workspace and say that it was time to smoke, and so often everyone smoked whenever just one person wanted to smoke.

John didn't smoke well. He held cigarettes wrong—not between the first two fingers, but usually between the thumb and first finger. He squinted when he inhaled. He never smoked in high school and barely smoked in college, so he was going against the tide. The trend was that people would, when they were young, thoughtlessly start smoking and then be unable to quit. Later, when they were a bit older, most people knew better, or had enough self-control, or sense, to not start smoking.

John's friends—both those who smoked and those who didn't—would always tell him to quit smoking.

But his friends still went outside to smoke with him. No one was sure yet really how to make people not smoke most effectively. What if you yelled at them every day? Or what if you cried and wailed every time they smoked? What if you put pictures of people dying from smoking on the walls of their office cubicles?

All or none of these things might work but, according to the Mayor, what did work was simply making cigarettes as close to unobtainable as possible. In the

City, cigarettes now cost no less than nine dollars for twenty cigarettes in a box. A new sixty-two-cent federal tax went into effect right then; this followed a raise, the year previous, in the state tax on cigarettes from one dollar and fifty cents to two dollars and seventy-five cents. All told, the taxes on a pack of cigarettes were now at five dollars and twenty-six cents. So this meant that the actual product's cost was mostly composed of tax, and then money for the producers of cigarettes, with a little bit being retained by the people who actually sold them. Or less than a little: This was why cigarettes were a minimum of nine dollars, because already some stores sold them for ten or eleven or twelve dollars. Soon they would be fifteen.

In other parts of the country, cigarettes were as cheap as four dollars a pack. But the Mayor said that, while fewer people were smoking all over the country, that in the City, even more people were smoking less. The problem was that he was right. He could personally afford all the cigarettes he wanted, but he didn't smoke at all. Instead he had his safer vices, like private planes, which were mildly dangerous, certainly less safe than planes maintained by big companies, and certainly created a lot of pollution to transport a single man, but certainly did not take away years of a person's life on average. Also one of his houses had a fifty-thousand-dollar snooker table that, maybe, he could accidentally walk into and injure himself.

ON A SUNDAY, John hung out with Jordan and Jeff. John had seen Jordan recently, but he hadn't seen Jeff in a long while. Jordan had, somehow, never before told Jeff that he had dated John, back in the day—and for so long!—and John had never cared that Jeff didn't know.

Now, after Jeff knew, he was just a little weird about John. Aggression, jealousy, self-recrimination: If you knew how to look at people the right way, you could see any of these things and more manifesting in microexpressions, in the veiled hostility of humor, the language of the body. But you had to be careful that you weren't projecting these emotions on people. People were as easy to misinterpret as they were to read. What could you see in Jeff turning his body to the side, the array of ways he touched Jordan, and the smiles most of all? Were the smiles false and teeth-baring, or were they sympathetic and brotherly?

Jordan was very tall and handsome and rather blond, with a deep chesty voice. When Jordan graduated from his professional school just a couple years back, right around the same time John did, he had total debt of around 160,000 dollars, only a little of which had been carried over from their undergraduate studies. The payment plan started around 1,200 dollars a month, on a thirty-year basis, which he could afford, because he made a good bit of money. The debt built, over time, with interest. The most economically rational idea, he thought, was to pay the minimum and invest the rest, to outpace the interest. But that proved too complicated. Instead he paid more than was required, to chip away at the always-growing interest, and so he had no savings whatsoever.

He did not like his job at all. That wasn't something he had the luxury to think about.

Jordan had seen, in this museum in another country, called the Musées royaux des Beaux-Arts de Belgique, this old painting that people then thought was by an artist called Brueghel. In the painting, all gold and blue in the center, there's a bay, and a leg sticking out of the water, and a farmer plowing on the shore, head down, and a traveling man or a shepherd with a dog, with his back to the person who's fallen into the water, and there's also a schooner sailing away. A poet named Auden wrote about it once: "How everything turns away / Quite leisurely from the disaster; the ploughman may / Have heard the splash, the forsaken cry, / But for him it was not an important failure." A poem was like a story, but more abstract. This poem was about how something amazing and terrible was happening right in front of someone on an ordinary day but there was work to perform. Without the work there would be no crop. Without the crop there would be no rent, or no dinner, or some other kind of trouble. That's exactly like the human reaction to other people's tragedies—still, now—Jordan thought, what with all the people having lost their jobs. They have more important things going on. You can be adjacent to other people's misery, but misery had to be right on top of you for it to matter. Jordan felt like his behavior now, in the middle of it all, was like that.

He had looked at research about human happiness and believed that people weren't really good judges of what made them happy. He was in the City because he had lived in other cities and didn't enjoy them, and his friends were there, and his family was near, and so it should make him happy. But also things were going disastrously everywhere. For instance, now his dad made less money than he'd made in twenty-five years. And still Jordan wondered: How is the state of the world going to affect my bonus pay, come the end of the year? In the grand scheme of things, other people at that time were facing legitimate catastrophes—the loss of their homes, the evaporation of their savings—and Jordan wasn't. Most of the people in his graduate school class from just a few years previous were employed, while the ones graduating now from the same schools were not, and maybe never would be. But he also thought there was a bigger crisis yet to come. Jordan had a certain amount of envy of people who were maybe struggling a little more financially at the moment but were good at what they were pursuing. Was this fair? He figured it absolutely wasn't, but he still felt that way anyway. Other people were doing something they wanted to do forever, that they cared about. He thought that they went to bed with a sense of satisfaction, while he could not.

THIS WAS ABOUT right when the trees started to come back, because the seasons were still so regular. Plants were actually everywhere in the City, but always invisible until they began to emit a tiny green mist of new leaves. Soon enough the first brave woman would go outside in just a blouse or a tight T-shirt, while doing laundry, maybe, on a Sunday. A wave would ripple across the City, boys in skinny jeans and well-worn T-shirts that didn't cover their chicken-thin hips. Chest hair! Again! The backs of knees were shining everywhere. There was maybe no good evolutionary or biological reason for everyone to want to touch someone's skin on that first warm day of spring, but there it was. The days came a bit too cold or a bit too hot, like a patient with a fever, unpredictable. The nights grew more tempting. The mornings were easy, until the day came when you woke up, your throat swollen, the apartment too hot and gross, before the cold spell of the open window. The trees would stop and just wait. The looping squiggly bands of air would get pushed and bunched around the world, and then finally one day a warm dry blast settled along every avenue and abandoned lot. The City transformed. Bright green leaves lined the park fences, surrounded the shrieks of the playground fights. The streets were transformed with the lines of greenery, reflecting the boxes of blocks and buildings, elegant or scraggly or malformed or patchy, but at least reaching, some even flowering. A few came busting out in a pink glaze, set against jewel-box green. It was coming, time and date unknown, but always it would get there, the full shrinking of the night, the hot juicy wetness of the days.

THE MAYOR CAME out and made a speech that took everyone by surprise. "I don't want to walk away from a city I feel I can help lead through these tough times," he said. And:

We live in a world where, normal course of business, companies and individuals borrow money and repay it. And that process has come to a stop. And that's a much more difficult thing to work out of. Why people lose confidence and why people gain confidence, psychologists get PhD theses trying to figure that out. But they are long-term swings and I don't think anybody questions that we have a problem. . . .

I will say that we are better prepared than we could have been. We have for the last couple of years, as you know, kept saying, the good times can't go on forever. . . . Some of our largest employers and most established companies are in turmoil—and others don't even exist anymore. . . . We may well be on the verge of a meltdown, and it's up to us to rise to the occasion. . . .

As our economic situation has become increasingly unstable, the question for me has become far less about the theoretical and much more about the practical. And so, to put it in very practical terms, handling this financial crisis while strengthening essential services such as education and public safety is a challenge I want to take on for the people. . . .

On the same day, the head of the City Council came out and said that they would be introducing legislation to repeal the two-term limit law, which meant that the Mayor would be clear to run for office for a third time. She said that the decision would be made in a week. "The Mayor has made very clear that he wants the City Council to consider legislation that will extend term limits from eight to twelve years. We will obviously do that. Each person will have to stand up and vote yes or no," she said. This did not make a whole lot of sense on the face of it. The people of the City had voted twice, as a group, to not allow mayors to serve more than two terms. But then the Mayor had "made very clear" what he wanted, and he was used to getting what he wanted.

Two of the City's living previous mayors came forward to endorse the Mayor for this third term. The other did not.

JOHN'S BOSS CALLED all of the staff into the conference room. It was a bright white room. He was going to quit, Thomas said. He couldn't protect them from the owner anymore, he said.

"Are you leaving us for another woman?" one woman asked.

He didn't want anyone talking about this in public, he said. "If anyone leaks this before we're willing to announce this, I'm going to be bullshit," he said. Everyone looked around at each other in the white room. He meant "batshit," everyone realized. "Bullshit" meant something that was aggressively false. "Batshit" meant crazily angry.

Right before he'd come into the meeting, Thomas had taken a phone call from a woman with a website. "I can't talk to you right now!" he'd said to her. "I'm about to go into a meeting and announce that I'm quitting!"

And so while they were in the meeting, she'd written about this on her website. So when everyone eventually stumbled out of the conference room, it was already done and everyone knew, thereby, at least, putting no one in the awkward position of having to tell people themselves.

TWELVE YEARS BEFORE John was born, the country renounced a policy that tied its paper currency to actual reserves of gold. The country had maintained a set price for gold—thirty-five dollars an ounce, which is what citizens were paid in exchange for the gold that they were, for a time, no longer allowed to own. Other countries held their own currencies tied to an exchange rate of the country's "dollar." A good chunk of the powerful world was in league—briefly.

The name "dollar"—the name for a currency unit equal to one—supposedly came about from the "thaler," a currency name dating from another continent, hundreds of years ago. The dollar coin was first defined as twenty-something grams of pure silver, according to a statesman ages ago; that amount of silver, however, was reduced twice and then, eventually, no silver at all was put into silver dollar coins.

While the coins were made of silver, the paper version of the dollar represented gold. But soon, the government had many more "dollars" in the world than it had gold. To pay some debts, it made a great deal many more "dollars." And then: The countries in league with the U.S. currencies demanded that their debts be redeemed in actual gold instead of some paper that represented gold.

So the government told them that the deal was off.

Money, untethered, was never the same. The little flat bills became potent objects. To burn this paper, or to deface this paper, was a crime. To create fake versions of this paper, which many people did, was an even greater crime. But why wouldn't they? It had all the value, and it was far easier to counterfeit than some soft metal that had come slamming in from the sky and then had melted into the rock of the planet.

THE OWNER OF John's company bought himself a new place to live. The people who were selling it wanted 3.5 million dollars for it, but he paid only 3.2 million dollars for it. It had two bedrooms, and was two thousand square feet, and had a metal staircase that led from the public or entertaining spaces downstairs to the private spaces upstairs. The bedroom upstairs had a window that was the top half of a circle, and was surrounded by an arch of bricks. All the other windows were normal and rectangular though.

AFTER THOMAS QUIT, John and Sally and also Trixie and Trixie's husband and some others from work were sitting in Duke's, a terrible restaurant that was a few blocks from the office. Duke's was a restaurant that was all dressed up in fake things from outside of the City, but not exotic, foreign things; instead they were homey, supposedly nostalgic things. Like street signs and funny pictures and the license plates of old cars from other states and red-and-white-checkered tablecloths, reminiscent of a church social. Like it was supposed to be exciting because it was strange and therefore transporting, but really it was bleak.

They were very upset. It was like someone had died. It was a vague instability made explicit. They talked about if it all made sense. Was it okay that dealing with the owner had become too onerous or, at least, not worth their boss's time? Or was it just not worth the money to him? What did it mean that he'd said he didn't feel like he could protect people anymore? So then who would, when the owner wanted to carve up the staff, to "cut costs," to "keep the company lean," just like every other company they knew, where all their friends had lost their jobs? And what about the owner's point of view? The owner, for his part, thought the boss was slow and stodgy, unwilling to live in the real world of money.

Everyone was thinking about who was going to lose his job. The idea, the maybe-fact, that everyone thought they understood, that had likely been relayed from their boss to Timothy, or through some other channel of gossip, was that three hundred thousand dollars a year at least had to be cut from the budget. That probably meant that the newer hires, the people who'd come on in the last year, would all go. Or who knew? Some of those people were making fifty thousand dollars a year; some were making more, some less. You never knew how much people were making, even if they sat right next to you, unless you had a serious talk and compared notes or spied on their pay stubs, and there were strong cultural prohibitions against both those things. Three hundred thousand dollars a year could mean eight people; it could mean four people.

In any event, their boss had quit.

John and Sally went outside. They smoked.

"It's going to be okay," Sally said.

"Fuck, fuck, fuck," John said. "No, it's not."

She'd never seen him like this.

JOHN HAD BEEN not-sleeping with a guy also named John. They would do things like go out to dinner, a kind of pretend dating, but they hadn't slept together. So this other John had a birthday party, at a bar called the Phoenix. The Phoenix was a bar in the sense that it had lively music and also a bar with bartenders behind it, and other than that was pretty much just a room that was a weird shape, with brick walls and some stools.

One of John's other friends was visiting for the occasion, from a less interesting country. "How has your trip been?" John asked.

"Obviously I've been a huge slut, I've slept with someone every day," the foreigner said. The foreigner was wearing a slot machine sweatshirt, which is to say, a sweatshirt with a slot machine pictured on it.

"That sounds like fun," John said, meaning the opposite.

"Obviously I'm not as big a slut as John," the foreigner said, meaning the other John, the one that John was not really dating.

"Oh really?" John said, all interested now.

"Yeah, he's slept with like four guys in the last five days," the foreigner said.

Good to know, John thought.

Across the room John could see a friend, a mopey guy who never had much to say. His hair was always overstylized, in that it was designed to fall over his eyes. He was talking to this other boy—this really dramatically cute boy that John had heard about. Friends had always said to him, over and over, John, you have to meet this guy, you guys would really get along. Oh, we'll really get along? John asked. No, not like that, he's basically married, everyone said.

But John had seen pictures of him on Facebook. There was one of this guy with a friend where they were walking in the rain and he was so skinny and he had a buzz cut and a weird but very pretty face and he was smoking a cigarette.

No way I'm saying hello to him first, John thought. He can say hello to me. So he turned his back.

"Hey, John, you know Amy, right?" the mopey guy later came over to say.

"Yup," John said.

"My friend Edward here is Amy's best friend," he said. "You should talk about Amy."

And so John finally turned to Edward.

"I'm not interested in Amy," John said to Edward, and he got up close. "I'm interested in you."

Edward's back was up against a gumball machine. They talked. Edward was agitated and lively and nervous and excited. When they at last looked around, most everyone was long gone, except for Fred, a school friend of John's, shambling by.

"John, I gotta get outta here," Fred said.

"Yeah, you know, I guess I should go too?" Edward said.

John leaned in. "I'd really like it if you stayed for another drink," he said.

"I'm going to stay for another drink," Edward said and ran his hands through his hair.

Fred walked out oblivious.

They talked about where they lived. Edward lived not far away. "Oh, that's so much closer, we should just go over there," John said.

"I should tell you," Edward said, just out the door. "I have a boyfriend."

John clapped his hands. Right.

"He's, like, on vacation," Edward said. "Right now he's not home."

"So, shall we?" John said.

"Uh, okay," Edward said.

They walked the mile back to Edward's place. Well, really: They went back to Edward's boyfriend's place.

SOMETIMES WORK WAS just what you clocked into while you were falling in love. Sometimes sex was just something you did while you weren't at work. Drugs were something you did sometimes when you couldn't deal with one of those things, or with yourself. The City was so expensive and so grueling sometimes that it was easy to be unsure why you were there. Many were there to make money, money that could largely only be made there, in the long spiny arms of industries that could never grow anywhere else or anywhere smaller. Some people just liked it, its loudness and crowdedness and surprises. Some started there for a reason and then couldn't imagine being anywhere else, but maybe lost track of that reason along the way. Some people had a plan. Some were just chancing it. Either way the months flew by, and over the years you came up with something or you came up with not much.

WORK THE NEXT day was a disaster. John was exhausted. The office was tense. John went over to a bookshelf and threw everything on the ground.

Then he calmed down, went back to his computer, chatted with Fred.

Fred, you'll never guess what happened. I slept over at Edward's.

You crashed there?

No, I slept with him.

I don't mean this the wrong way, but I'm actually really shocked.

John thought this was the meanest thing Fred had ever said.

Gee, thanks, Fred, John wrote.

No no no, Fred wrote, not because it doesn't seem like the right match, but because Edward is religious about not doing anything with anybody.

And then . . . nothing happened. John was going nuts. Nothing was straight in his head and he checked Edward's Twitter, which was like Facebook—people wrote things there on the Internet in public, but shorter. And it said something like, "Feeling gloomy tired and worn out today." And John nearly burst into tears.

John talked to Chad about it. Chad was like, "Well, uh, he just cheated on his boyfriend?"

Well, if you want to think about it like that, John thought.

So John wrote Edward an email. Subject line: "Now." Body: "That was fun."

Edward wrote back, in total: "Yes it was. . . . xo"

And John thought, Oh crap. And then, kind of desperately, he wrote back something chatty and overtired and Edward didn't even respond.

Later that day, after consulting with his work friends, he wrote an email to Edward.

"Hey, I don't want to screw anything up for you but I'd love to see you again." He wrote that he meant "just as friends."

Half an hour later he got two emails. One said, Edward has added you as a friend on Facebook. The other said, yeah, I think that's a great idea to be friends, my boyfriend's an awesome guy, everything that happened—

John stopped reading.

NOT THAT LONG before, two businessmen perfected an idea that they had been kicking around for quite some time. They made a company that extended credit, on behalf of an individual, that was accepted at an array of stores. Since before the invention of money, it was common for people to delay the payment side of a transaction. For instance: He gives her a dead bird, presumably for eating, but doesn't ask for payment right away; tomorrow, after being paid the shells due her for a woven basket, she gives him the shells that she owes him for the bird.

This was called credit, and in modern times, what

these men invented was called a charge card. The card was a signifier that one held money; the holder of the card would pay the issuer of the card at the end of the month; the issuer of the card would pay the stores at which the person had received goods or services.

So people, particularly people who did not have many "dollars" on hand, could borrow automatically, through these cards, in exchange for paying the total amount due at the end of the month.

It was not long—not even ten years—after that that there came the credit card. With the credit card, the holder was not compelled to pay the money due at the end of the month. Instead, in exchange for allowing the holder to retain the money he or she had spent, the issuer of the card—a bank—would simply charge the card user "interest."

"Interest" was such a funny word to be chosen to mean this. "Interest" was an old, old word, first meaning "to concern," later meaning "to draw the attention of" and also "cognizance for one's own earnings"—and in this case it meant essentially that, if there was an outstanding "balance," then the issuer of the credit card would increase the amount that was owed.

Interest was usually expressed as a percentage; it could range from almost nothing to as high as in the hundreds.

What kind of rate one was given was, at least in part, based on how well—but not too well—one behaved with other credit cards. For instance, never paying money owed was a very bad thing. Never borrowing money at all was a less bad thing, but still not a good thing, in the eyes of financial institutions. Always paying some was considered the best thing of all.

In a sense, interest was insurance for the bank. There would always be people who would not pay, after all, so the interest earned from others would offset those losses.

But also there was money to be made there. For instance, some cards had fees just for users to be allowed to have them. Some cards started with a very low "interest" rate that then jumped dramatically. There were also "late fees," for any tardiness in payment.

Eventually it became necessary for the government to intervene on behalf of credit card users. Just then, laws were enacted that said credit card companies could not, for instance, dramatically raise the interest rates on cards without allowing people to continue paying off what they owed at the prior rate. The government had to mandate that monthly due dates for payments could not fall on a day on which mail was not delivered. The government had to declare that cardholders could, when they had multiple cards with the same issuer, first pay off the account with the highest interest; previously the credit card companies had declared that any payments would be applied to the lowest-interest card first.

Just six companies were responsible for issuing four out of every five credit cards. At around this time, all the credit cards in the country had about 950 billion dollars in debt piled upon them, spread between about 150 million people. In the year previous, all kinds of fees—late fees, over-the-"limit" fees, annual fees—were thought to total 20 billion dollars.

AT A BOOK party a week after Edward and John met—that is, a party to celebrate a book—a friend of Amy's came up to John and said, hey, wow, Edward really, really likes you. And John was elated.

Later John would find out that Edward wrote that stupid thing on Twitter about being sad only because it was raining outside. Edward had actually never been happier in his life.

IN THE END, the elected members of the City Council, after hearing from the public, were compelled to decide whether the Mayor could run for the third time, and the vote went 29 in favor to 22 opposed. This was, apparently, legal, even if it seemed like it shouldn't be. "Our City is facing the worst fiscal crisis since the Great Depression," the head of the City Council said. The Great Depression was the last great contagion, eighty years previous. Her implication was that continuity in leadership would help prevent things getting worse. She planned on being the mayor herself after the current Mayor's third term.

Most everyone felt dimly outraged—some more than dimly. In the council chambers, after the vote, people were actually screaming from the balconies. But then what? Not enough people were so outraged as to go and do—well, what? March on the Mayor's house? People had to go to work, after all. Also there were so many good things on their TVs.

EDWARD WAS BEING cagey, but finally John convinced Edward to get together for drinks, at the Nowhere Bar, a red-tinted basement bar, dark and campy and not far from Edward's place, or, that is to say, Edward and Edward's boyfriend's place. It was more than a week but less than two weeks after they had met. They were having a lot of fun! John was so happy to see him. They sat next to each other in the dark, and the glow of their faces was all there was.

I may be moving back down to the Capital soon, Edward said, to my parents' house. John grabbed his arm. You can't do that, you can't leave town, he said. And Edward said, you know we can't do this, right?

And John said, why not? And Edward said, because I'm fucked up. And I love my boyfriend.

And yet. Edward was really effusive too. He said that he really liked John. But what were they supposed to do, exactly? Edward asked. He said he'd seen a number of friends leave their boyfriends for another person, and look what happened. It never worked.

So they went their own ways.

After this night, John kept harassing Edward online, flirting, chatting . . . but then he was faced with this chill, and he did back off. He didn't want to be a complication, exactly, because actually he did like Edward. He didn't want him in trouble or in torment.

John and Kevin and a bunch of others went to see Edward at a bar right before he left to go live with his parents for a while, to send him off. John intentionally didn't look at Edward the whole night.

And at the end of that night, Kevin said to John, it is so hilarious how all you do is stare at Edward and all Edward does is stare at you.

I wasn't even looking at him! John said. And Kevin said, please, all you do is stare at each other longingly.

So John came up to Edward right before he left. Well,

I'll be down your way pretty soon myself for a weekend, he said. I'll come see you maybe. Would you like that?

THE CITY'S OWNERS were its engine, a kind of smaller city within the City, and they flatly served its purposes, to amass organizations that made and also spent capital. To do so they needed a few segments of population. So it served to have all these various layers of people: the people to work in the offices, the people to clean the offices, the people to buy and sell the offices, the people to feed the people within the offices, and the people to feed the people who owned the offices. Everyone else was a kind of gray noise while the credit card numbers bounced from tower to tower, transaction to transaction. Some people's entire lives were nothing but the reverberations of this noise! "Leisure time" was spent consuming, handing over hours of one's day to someone's corporate entity. This was a fair trade. It must be said that people wanted it that way or they wouldn't have been converting their dollars into products.

And also this was the attraction of the City: the proximity of the plates of classes grinding together, the corner office visible from the bullpen. When someone was young in the City, he couldn't know what he would be, and that was an alluring mystery. Some days he might think he was bound for riches too. Some hours he might think he was slipping into a permanent disaster.

And everything else that was free, the people you spoke with and the people you slept with, those were strategies of filling a need you could not address in a system of capital. Which is to say, the good news was that no matter how hard the City tried, or the owners in the City tried, it could not make absolutely everything about profit and need.

People's lives would always seep out toward freedom, trashy or hilarious or messy or sexy or whatever—toward things that lie beyond profit and loss and order and economy.

ONE NIGHT CHAD said, I'll be downtown, let's hang out. And John said, great, I'll be with Fred. So they met up at the Magician, the worst place, a terrible plain little bar where John and his coworkers went after work and drank too much, where tonight Diego's friends were hanging out. When John got there, one of Chad's friends, Dan, was storming out of the bar. And Chad was running after him, yelling, wait, wait, Dan!

And John was like, whoa, hello. And: Slow down, can you explain what's happening? And Chad said, it's all my fault, but apparently one of Diego's friends wanted a really low-key evening, where it was just her and her friends hanging out, and so I offered Dan a free table nearby so you guys could sit there.

So John said, come sit with us, Dan, who cares. He didn't even want to sit with Diego and his college friends. Fred joined them at their side table, away from everyone, and they spent most of the time talking about how they thought Diego was bizarrely mean to them. John said so first, and Dan said, oh, you too? Hmm! Every time they'd get into it, Chad would come by and they'd quickly start talking about sports. Diego had what John thought was a crazy new haircut that was shaved on the sides and long on top, and John went by to say, hey, nice haircut.

The night wound down. Diego's friends were walking out. And Diego stopped by their table and said, John, what's going on with your hair?

What do you mean? John asked.

And Diego said, it's just really ridiculous right now. And your five o'clock shadow? And your hair? It's really, really disconcerting.

John's whole face tightened and he said, well, you look great. And Diego said, I dunno, John. And then: Well, I hope you're coming to this Saturday birthday party we're having.

Oh, we'll definitely be there, John said. Chad was all

aquiver in anxiety. They left. Thank God you were the bigger man, Dan and Fred said. Really? John said. Because I found his gut disconcerting.

The following Tuesday, he had drinks with Chad. How's your capacity for a difficult subject? John asked. Well, I dunno, said Chad. Okay, here's the deal, I never want to see your boyfriend again, John said. Chad was really good about it. Diego really likes you! Chad said. I will listen to whatever you tell me, John said. If you tell me I'm an overly sensitive asshole, that's fine. Let's table this, Chad said, and I will talk to him subtly. And I'll do whatever you want, John said. John actually hated Diego at this point, but he was making something of an attempt. Maybe he was a little mad that he was thinking about Edward all the time, and Edward was floating there just out of reach, and here was a pair of lovers, and it was nowhere near as good, or so he thought.

JOHN WAS ON the highway, on his way down to the Capital, and he got an email on his phone. It was from Edward: "Are you still coming down?" He was driving down with his coworker Rex. And John asked Rex, do we even have time? And should I even see him? Well yeah, you should definitely go see him, Rex said. Rex was secretly deep, John thought.

So John had dinner with his friends that night, and afterward went outside to smoke and wait for Edward, who eventually showed up wearing a purple deep-V shirt and torn jeans, a very funny outfit. John was in a suit. He jumped into Edward's parents' white minivan. Where are we going to go? he asked. And Edward said, well, we can go to the sports bar or we can go somewhere else. Somewhere else, John said. No, I'm taking you to the sports bar, Edward said. It's called Nellie's and it has an outdoor smoking section. John had already turned off the part of him that was into Edward, he thought, but they spent an hour at the bar and had so much fun and fast talk and it was all corny, laughing, brain-chemical crush. They went from one side of the bar to the other. Every guy is checking you out, Edward said. But there's only one guy I'm here with, that I'm interested in, John said. Then it was two a.m. and the bar was closing. John had been drinking seltzer all night. Edward was drinking though. Well, alright, I guess I'll drive you back to where you're staying, Edward said. And it was time to say good night. So what are you doing now? John asked. Oh, I'm going to go watch movies in my parents' rec room, Edward said. Well, I wish you'd told me that earlier, John said, I would have watched movies in your parents' rec room. Well, you can if you want, Edward said. How about this? John said. I have to go back to where I'm staying, I have a ton of work stuff to do down here, and I have to get up early, but tell you what, why don't you pick me up tomorrow and we'll go watch movies in your parents' rec room.

John got through the next day and a long night of work. John messaged Edward: Wanna come pick me up? So Edward showed up in the dark in the white minivan. John got in. Hey, kid, it's good to see you, John said and touched the back of his head. His hair was wet. Did you just take a shower? John said. Well maybe, Edward said. Oh okay, John said. They went off to suburbia, a fifteen-minute ride, and Edward made him laugh. They passed a girl not wearing very much walking down the street, and Edward said, oh, this town's really in transition. They got back to the dark house and they smoked in the backyard. Edward's parents and his grandmother were asleep upstairs. They went down to the basement. There were wood-paneled walls and a little TV. So we can watch one of two movies, Edward said. We can watch *Back to the Future* or *Real World: Season One*.

Real World: Season One, John said. John took his tie and his coat off and spread across the couch. I'm so tired, he said. And John turned and Edward was staring at him. Look at you, he said. Then Edward pounced on him.

They fell asleep on this couch. Suddenly Edward was shaking him. It was five twenty in the morning.

"Well, we can do one of two things. You can stay over, though I don't know what my dad would think of that, or I can drive you back," Edward said.

"How long was I sleeping for?" John asked.

"Like forty-five minutes," Edward said.

"Were you asleep too?" John asked.

"No," Edward said.

"Were you just sitting here paranoid, staring out the window?" John asked.

"No, I was just sitting here in a total reverie. I'm so happy," Edward said.

"Well, you can drive me back," John said.

THE OWNER OF John's company fired the cleaning lady who came around each night and emptied the trash cans and vacuumed and did everything. Who would clean now?

AT THAT TIME, it wasn't customary to ask other people for money. That was one reason why credit cards were so successful, so universal. It was considered better to borrow from strangers, at an interest rate, than from friends. But the closer you were to a person, generally, the more acceptable it was to ask someone for a "loan." If you were very close, sometimes someone would even give you some money, as a present. Plus the laws said that if you died, your money would go to your spouse, and if you didn't have one, it would go to your closest blood relative.

But to borrow money from friends regularly was definitely frowned upon. Timothy, John's manager at work, asked people who worked for and with him for money sometimes as often as every two weeks. No one understood where his money went. Bosses were paid more money than nonbosses by the owner of the corporation because of the idea that the further up the supervisory ladder you were, the more money you should make. Although maybe not much? Someone in the office said it was because Timothy put all his money in a retirement account. No one actually knew, and it wasn't anyone's business, and some people didn't mind at all. The people at the company were all close, at least in part because the quarters were close. Some of the people who worked together even loved each other. And they all liked the idea of being able to loan each other money! But, for most of them, money regularly stood a chance of running out, so they weren't in a position to give or loan too freely. This was a situation of some or even great anxiety: trying to balance one's goodwill with one's own self-maintenance.

Little loans of course weren't a big deal. One night, John was on a random date, and at the end of it, he realized he was totally out of money. He called a nearby friend, at one in the morning, for cab fare home. The friend had just laughed and left twenty dollars downstairs with his building's doorman. But also the friend thought that this was evidence of something: poor planning, maybe. People believed that having no money reflected on a person's character, even in little ways.

Almost all companies distributed pay twice a month instead of all at once. If people quit or were fired, the company would obviously be protected from having to recover some of the "unearned" salary. And it would involve too much paperwork, for one thing, to pay employees more often than that.

To run out of money, even for just the two days before "payday," felt like raw panic, like the end of everything. That time stretched out, and the worst anxiety was then that you had to ask for one of these loans.

To have no money and nowhere to get more meant that it was nearly impossible to focus on anything else. One would feel giddy, or anxious, or sad, or manic, or sleepy, or even exhausted, but one couldn't avoid the dread of the next thing going wrong. For instance, these shortfalls meant perhaps a shortfall in the payments one owed: less important, for cable TV or water, or more important, for rent. These people couldn't stop thinking about it, when they maybe saw some food that they wanted to buy, or when they had to walk someplace, or maybe when they were thinking about their future, or even when they were doing something that had no price at all.

EDWARD HAD SLEPT with a lot of people in high school and was glad he did so he could say he had. But he was a little jealous of what he thought of as John's checkered love life. It wasn't about the sex, he wasn't jealous of that. For him sex was somewhat about wanting people to like you, so usually he was happy with someone just conveying interest. When Edward went to bars with John, it was like John was a superhero who had a weird sixth sense, an omniscience. It was like John was viewing the bar from above: That guy was going to the bathroom, but if you could catch him on the way out, he'd go home with you. He could suss out every dynamic in the room and understand everybody's inner workings and everyone's rhythms and he was always right. And then he could turn an intensity on a person, like a blinding light in the dark.

Edward was completely unprepared for this kind of attention the night they met. He realized that he was a completely easy mark. Edward could count on one hand the number of times he'd gone home with someone from a bar. John wasn't his type even. But Edward never dated guys who were his type; his real type was young, skinny, hairless. None of that mattered—he didn't even know why he was thinking about it! Two people had that pull, that warming reaction; they made something new together by being together, or they didn't, and if you really did, it was impossible to set aside.

THE MAYOR GAVE a speech about the recent state of things. It was less than six months before the election. The Mayor said that people were spending money again. "In fact I'm reasonably optimistic that we've turned the corner," he said. When asked why, then, the Mayor still thought that he should be allowed a third term, he did not answer the question and in fact called the question asker "a disgrace."

The week prior, 623,000 people in the country reported being newly unemployed, and the total number of people receiving unemployment insurance payments from the government had hit a record—for the seventeenth straight week in a row.

It was unclear what corner was being turned. While he was the Mayor, the number of poor people in the City had grown as well: 1.6 million people in the City were now considered poor. That was 20.1 percent of everyone who lived in the City.

There was at least one small plan from the Mayor to help change that. He got a number of other rich people to give money, and they paid a group of poor people small amounts of money to do good things, like keep their children in school and see doctors. For instance, if a child passed an annual school exam or improved his score from a previous year, the child's parents would get 300 dollars. Or if they went for an annual checkup with a doctor, they'd get 200 dollars. If a parent kept a full-time job, she or he would get 150 dollars a month. At the end of this program, an enrolled family had on average some savings—about 575 dollars. Two out of three families said they thought they were better off afterward. And only three out of five of them were still technically poor.

There was also a surprise finding to this experiment. Compared with similar people in the City who were not in this program, more of the single people in this program got married. People said they felt like they could commit to being in a permanent relationship when they felt financially secure.

EDWARD MADE A sudden trip up to the City. He and John planned to meet at Metropolitan. Fred showed up. And Edward brought his friend Jason. John was so excited to see Edward, he didn't really notice Jason. Jason was handsome, and had no hair, and he was shiny and trim. He gave off a sense of being a pleasing series of little circles, from his glossy scalp to his big eyes to his round cheeks. Then when he smiled all the circles collapsed and he had a squint in his eyes that could cut glass.

He was really smart, really bright, and talked like Edward but was a bit more substantive, John thought. Well: Interested more in the sort of things John was interested in. Jason had a funny way of talking—his voice was sort of deep, but he had a habit of saying things like "Jinxies!" if you said things at the same time or "Drinksies!" if you were going to the bar.

Jason had been coupled-up his whole life; he'd met his first boyfriend at seventeen, and they'd been together until about a year ago, when Jason's ex just up and moved to the other coast. It was brutal.

So every time Jason went to the bathroom, John and Edward would touch each other and kiss a little. And every time Edward left, John and Jason would kiss and feel each other up. John decided he was going home with one of them and they could choose, or he would go home with both of them.

All the while, Fred was clapping his hands, laughing his head off.

And then Edward announced he was going home to

bed. And Jason left with him. So John didn't go home with either of them.

THE LAST WEEK of work came for John's boss. He'd become more and more absent, and finally he wasn't there anymore.

Timothy, who had been basically the number two, would take over the office for the owner. Timothy saw his ascension as a way to minimize what he saw as the harm that the owner wanted to do to the office. There was much dramatic strategizing. There was much scheming over drinks. There were hushed conversations outside, and people disappearing into offices, the doors closing slowly.

Timothy said he had to hurt some people to save everyone else. Across the bullpen and even a bit into the offices, people were going to be discarded. Timothy tried to solicit what business people called "buy-in" from the staff. He talked them through it. They sort of believed what he was saying, that if they sacrificed a few, that the office at large would be safe. He was very smart, and incredibly articulate; he was such a talker, and everyone liked him, so the things he said made sense. They tried to prepare themselves to take it "for the team." This was a projected idea, a way of looking at things that, through force of character, could be made an article of faith. Those that thought they were not going to be "laid off" felt good about this plan, which then made them feel bad for being selfish.

JASON CHATTED AT John. He'd gotten the contact info off Facebook or something. He told John he'd be at Metropolitan later. They met up, they made out. Chad showed up. Chad asked John if he could sleep over instead of schlepping all the way back home. Of course, John said. Forty minutes later, he said, sorry, Chad, no, you can't, actually.

What do you think? John asked. They were looking at Jason.

Oh, I'd be all over that if I were single, Chad said.

Okay! John said.

He and Jason took a cab back to John's. Jason even slept over and got brunch the next day.

"So you're not planning on telling Edward? We can just be friends?" Jason asked.

"Oh thank God, yes," John said. "Okay, we can be friend-os."

So they'd hang out at bars. Edward wasn't around, after all. And when they'd go out, there were a couple nights he was tired and he'd crash at Jason's place. And he'd sleep in the bed, but they wouldn't touch each other. They were becoming friends.

Then they went out one night to some trashy bar, with Fred, and John was all revved up and they played Mariah Carey's "All I Want for Christmas Is You." And Jason was trying to say something to John, in that late-night-drunk way. "Do you think, I dunno, whatever"—all these false starts. And John said, what are you saying, and Jason said, I don't know! And then, eventually, he coughed up something: It was that he had a brewing crush on John, maybe, he thought, just a little maybe, it was no big deal, but he had to say something.

John lied to Jason a little. "Of course I have feelings for you too, but things are really complicated right now," he said. He didn't know which thing to say: Should he be insulting, to make him go away? Or conciliatory? And what was true anyway? But John said, you know I have a lot of feelings for your best friend, right? And Jason said, I know. And: I wasn't asking for this or anything.

THEIR BOSS'S GOING-AWAY party was held at the enormous and relatively ancient building of a private club, in the shadows of the tallest part of the City. It was all marble and looked like a mausoleum. Really, it was only about 165 years old. Twenty years ago, the club had been forced to admit women as members. They had not wanted women there, for the simple reason that the members didn't want to associate with women.

It was a party that felt like a funeral. All the men put on ties. All the women put on high heels. People made speeches and everyone was anxious. The big main ground-floor room of the club absorbed all the people in the room so that, between the murmuring sound of cocktails being made and people talking, it still felt empty and cold and bright.

Also, no one knew who would be fired the next morning.

Some people drank too much, and so in the office the next morning—a Friday, because it had become traditional that groups of people should be fired on a Friday, so that people's feelings could cool and settle over the weekend—those people felt a bit chafed or unsteady. Some people brought bags with them in case they needed to pack their belongings.

They'd gotten advice from their friends at other companies about how to get fired.

That morning people sat at their desks doing nothing. It was raining miserably outside, if you looked through the windows of the offices.

Eventually people were summoned into their boss's old

office. It still looked like his office—books piled everywhere, a mess, a view of the skyscraper across the way—
but it didn't feel like his office with him gone. Timothy
and a representative of the owner, a man with a vampire
grin, met with people in the office. They had a stack of
folders prepared, one for each person they were going
to dismiss. People who came in couldn't see the other
people's names on the folders—they were careful about
that.

They fired the first few people. No one came out
crying. Everyone else sat in the bullpen anxiously. One
guy, Mark, was cleaning out his desk preemptively. In the
bottom of his desk, he found a strange thing left behind
from some previous employee who'd used the desk before
him. It was a plastic bib, designed to be tied around the
neck, that covered one's shirt while one was eating. This
bib was specifically intended for the eating of lobster, a
hard-shelled sea creature that you cooked and then broke
open, usually with tools. It was once considered something gross that poor people ate but was then an expensive delicacy. The bib had a picture of a lobster on it. It
also had the words "Let's get crackin'" written across it.
Mark put on the bib and tied it around his neck. It was
already midday, the layoffs had been proceeding all morning, and it was finally his turn to be called into the office.

He came in. There was a moment of quiet while Timothy and the man in the office considered the bib. Mark just sat there. He had succeeded in not being a good soldier, in making the moment as profoundly uncomfortable and as ludicrous as possible. They gave him his folder. He left the office and put his things in the bag he brought. He wrote some notes to his former coworkers and left them in envelopes. They were supposed to be supportive notes, well-wishing notes, but they were also a bit aggressive, even hostile in a few cases. Timothy offered to call a car for Mark, and Mark declined.

John helped Mark take his bag downstairs, and they waited in the heavy rain for a car for hire. The cabs kept passing by, and those that stopped wouldn't take him where he wanted to go. Mark yelled at a cabbie. Finally he got one and then he left and was gone forever, and John went back inside all wet to the broken office, where no one was doing any work at all. No one was even sure how many people had been let go. It was at least a dozen, everyone was sure. When people did the math, they knew the company had saved much more than three hundred thousand dollars. It was easily five hundred thousand. It could have been close to a million dollars. The math was all fuzzy and impossible to know. "Let's get crackin'," someone said in the bullpen. Eventually, they all just left for the day.

IT WAS FRED'S twenty-eighth birthday party. Chad met John at John's office, and they took the subway out to a neighborhood they didn't know well. They had to wait for a while. "There was a burst in the Lincoln Tunnel and traffic was backed up ninety minutes?" said Chad, recounting the news.

"There was a birth in the tunnel?" John asked.

"No, a burst!" Chad said. Chad was wearing shorts and an ungainly, oversize white tank top with strange, deeply scooped armholes.

They got off the train and walked out into the sun and wandered in what they thought was the right direction, up a rundown street with lots of islander BBQ joints and big long older cars, toward the bar where Fred was having his afternoon party. It was hot but pleasant, kind of dreamy.

That morning Fred had gone to the beach and was extra relaxed, which for him was very relaxed indeed. As they were looking for the bar, Fred shuffled through traffic toward them.

"Don't get hit!" said Chad.

"He's the kind of guy, Fred, the driver would get out of the car, apologize, and hand him the keys," John said to Chad.

Fred led them to the bar. "So are any of your interesting friends going to be there?" John asked.

Yes, the twenty-year-old that Fred was seeing would be there. And? "Tyler Flowers."

"Oh, he's very interesting," John said. John had met this Tyler once before and found him really attractive.

The bar was mostly like a long alley between two buildings, like a beer hall with picnic tables, mostly shady, and its cavernous inside areas were dark and empty.

John ordered a white wine and came back outside. Hardly anyone was there yet. "I had the shakes this morning, I was like Edward smoking," John said.

Soon enough Tyler showed up. Tyler was very thin, tall, gangly, with brown curly hair. He was in hipster jeans and big white sneakers and a thin faded flannel shirt and a braided belt. He had huge ears and skin like a glass of milk and was pretty. There was also something sort of ugly about him. Not ugly like he was a mean person, just there was something about his nostrils or the slope of his forehead that made him look like somewhat squished and frail. And his skin seemed so pale that you could see into his head a little.

John sprang into action and went to say hello. John was doing that thing where he smoked with his middle finger over on top of the cigarette and with his index finger beneath it. They talked for a while and then others showed up and horned in on Tyler. John gave up on his flirting for a while.

There were more drinks and time passed and a whole bunch of people showed up. Fred knew a lot of people. The main topic of conversation was Fred's upcoming move out of the country. Fred's departure had been some time coming, it had already been months since he'd first started talking about going, it was sort of like he had already left. In the way that people, when they know that someone's going to be leaving, protect themselves from a looming absence, they had already written off Fred. Years before this, all the leases in the City would expire on the same day of the year, and almost everyone would move at the same time. But because there was no Internet yet then, when you moved, you sometimes didn't see your friends again because they were too far and there were too few ways to keep in contact. So some people changed their friends every year. But at least now when Fred left the City, people could keep in touch with him fairly easily.

One of the women there had gone to professional school with Fred and John, but somehow she and John had never met. Everyone was talking about ordering food for delivery, in a lazy, slightly drunken yet definitely hungry way, and Chad got fed up with it and walked off to find a restaurant. Jason showed up.

After a really long time, Chad reappeared with his own food. Chad's burrito was disappearing down his gullet in huge, horrifying gulps.

"Oh my God, have you never seen Chad eat?" John asked the table.

A guy named Matt walked into the bar. He was a comedian, which meant that Matt performed in front of other people, for money, as often as was possible, in order to make them laugh. "I hate that guy so fucking much," Chad said. Disgusted, they watched Matt flirt with Tyler in the middle of the alley-patio.

"How a guy who studies baroque architecture"—for that is apparently what interested Tyler—"can talk to a guy who can only come up with skits about early onset diabetes is beyond me," Chad said, taking a break from his burrito.

"Let her rip!" John said. Chad was, in fact, just getting started. This weird thing happened where, instead of becoming exhausted by the onslaught of the burrito, something scary happened with his blood sugar and he got more and more manic.

Meanwhile, Matt and Tyler were deep in it. "I've never actually had sex like that!" Chad said. "It's like his penis is coming out the back of his head."

Fine, John thought. He was disillusioned, after Edward's refusal to be present, sort of angry, and to his mind relationships had become perhaps more transactional.

"You know what?" he said. "You're going to see the

comeback of the century. I feel like Hillary in New Hampshire right now."

"Your direct mail campaign is unparalleled," Chad said. "You're a long-term strategist. Hours? Days? No. It is months."

Diego showed up. Chad had gotten him a burrito too. Diego looked on sort of blankly while John was getting revved up to go steal Tyler away from Matt.

"You're the Neil Armstrong to his Christa McAuliffe," Chad said.

"I'm the Chamberlain to his Churchill," John said.

"Too soon!" Chad said.

Fred stumbled by, adorably. "Thank you for coming to my party!" he said. "Oh, I'm a little drunk!"

The party was full; it was unclear where it stopped and started and where the regular attendees of the bar began. A man showed up and took a seat at the edge of the picnic table where John and Chad were scheming. He had gotten a beer and now was reading an exceedingly obscure and storied intellectual journal. Some inexplicable sort of awkward moment happened that involved a recent arrival to the party: some boy who John had gone on one date with, who was now someone's paramour, and both Chad and John were expecting some drama, some awkwardness.

"And nothing cuts through awkward like John," Chad said.

"Like a hot knife through cheese!" John said.

"Like a hot knife through roast beef," Chad said. "Like a hot knife through Tyler Flowers."

"Hey, you want to see what a long-term strategy looks like?" John said, and then he got up and went to greet the recent arrival, who was just then talking to, yes, Tyler Flowers.

So he hugged the guy, who had a bunch of money in his hands. The guy looked awkward. "Oh hey, how are you," said the guy. Then John and the guy and Tyler Flowers were in a little conversational triangle.

"He is wading into a situation that one would normally avoid at all costs and that is his audacity," Chad said.

Chad sat and watched this all going on like it was on TV.

Then Matt, the sketch comic, came up and sidled into the triangle—right between John and Tyler.

John was telling a story. "Look at him, he looks like Rumsfeld in those meetings," said Chad.

There was incredible body language going on. For instance, John's body was ejecting the sketch comic from the group, by keeping a shoulder somewhat in front of the sketch comic and by turning directly toward Tyler.

"He has to deal with three people while subtly destroying two of them," Chad narrated.

Tyler was clutching a beer. The sketch comic now had one leg bent, using the knee next to John to form a barrier between John and Tyler Flowers.

John was talking, and the sketch comic was pressing his own pint glass viciously against his own face, in a strange and angry gesture. It was sharp-toothed animals in a tank. Then a fifth person entered the group, and polite introductions were made, and the tension evaporated and John saw that he was done. He rejoined Chad at the table.

"Ya gotta give 'em a break!" he said. Then: "Smokesies!" he said, mocking Jason.

Chad and John watched Tyler, apparently delighted by some new arrival. The sun had begun to set. Everyone had had more than a few. "You know what the problem is? He's too easy," John said, watching Tyler. "It's like Russian roulette. He could go home with him or him or him. I'm rather disappointed."

There was a young guy in some sort of soccer shirt and white, white pants, very flash and sporty. "You know who that guy is? A coin dealer," Chad said. "He just bought three million—in coins! He's like the owner of John's company, an 'independent real estate operator.' All on his own!" He said that sarcastically, meaning the opposite. At this time, the number-one predictor of future wealth was current wealth and, therefore, inherited wealth.

It was by now eight thirty p.m. The twenty-year-old NYU student that Fred was sleeping with showed up. Trevor was redheaded and pimply and dressed in what could only be described as a costume. Little tiny shorts and boots and a gray shirt with black pocket linings and sleeves and collar. He looked ridiculous yet brave.

"Only four and a half hours late," John said.

The kid came up and sort of mumbled at Chad, who was aggressively, rudely polite to him, and the kid mumbled something unintelligible, and then picked up a chair from the table and carried it over to where Fred was sitting.

It was now fully dark. Over by Chad, Matt the sketch comic was down on the ground, putting himself in the yoga posture called "side crow," balancing on both hands, elbows bent ninety degrees, his face toward the ground, his knees twisted to the side and supported on one elbow.

"God!" Chad shouted in disgust.

LATER THAT NIGHT, they went to Sugarland. Somehow, John started dancing with the little twenty-year-old, the one who was seeing Fred. It got very flirty, for no good reason. He was drunk. Well, they were all drunk.

And then that weekend John and Fred were in the park and John had gone to show some picture on his mobile phone to Fred, but the phone was open to Facebook, and there was a friend request from the twenty-year-old.

"What's that?" Fred asked. "Why?"

"Oh, I don't know, that's so weird!" John said.

IT WAS EASIER to not have a home in the summer than to not have a home in the winter, due almost entirely to the weather. Not having a place to live wasn't "bad" in itself. But people wanted to know why, and then they could say, "That is why you have no home, because you did that thing"—went to jail, or hurt someone, or became addicted to drugs, or went crazy—and then they could think that reason was why such a thing would never happen to them.

JOHN HAD A week of vacation. This was rare for him. As an employee, he was guaranteed a certain allotment of vacation days, something like ten of them a year. But it was pretty common practice for employers to discourage workers from actually using them. An employee would put in a request to use them on certain dates, and sometimes the boss or owner would tell the employee that they couldn't be spared then. It was also common for these earned vacation days to expire: that if you didn't use them within a certain amount of time, like within the calendar year, they were no longer available. There was also an arcane process through which, when employees worked on extra days, such as weekends or holidays, they were to accrue "comp time," and then they could use this to not work on workdays. In practice, this rarely happened. In any event, with the tension of the last two months, John hadn't had a vacation in ages, and Timothy did not deny him.

Instead of going somewhere out of the City, as was the usual practice, John stayed at home. Kevin took a night off from staying home to come out—he and Fred and John went to see an orchestra play for free in a park, and this night proved so much fun that they went to the Phoenix after.

At the bar they got beers, and Fred was flirting with some guy from overseas, and then Fred came over and whispered in John's ear: Tyler Flowers is here, with some guy. So John grabbed Kevin and threw him in the corner, and they started kissing urgently. I think Tyler saw us, Fred whispered into their joined faces. All night they ignored Tyler, and later, from home, John sent Tyler a message. Do you wanna get together? Yeah, that sounds like fun, what day works for you? Tyler asked. And then John realized he had no money to go out on a date and didn't even write him back.

In fact, John had run out of money quite completely. But he finally wrote back and told Tyler he was going to watch a tennis event on TV, at Sally's, with Rex and maybe some other people from work. It would be a "Wimbledon party." It wasn't so much a Wimbledon party as just them sitting there watching the Wimbledon men's finals on TV. Wimbledon was a prestigious annual tennis tournament held in another country, in which two very rich players would face off for a trophy and two checks: one big, for the winner, and one less big, for the loser. The winner got more than a million dollars. And Tyler said that sounded good. So the night before, Saturday night, John got a Facebook message from Tyler, and it said, I don't know if you were pulling my chain, but I'd really love to see you again and to go to your Wimbledon party. By then John had forgotten all about it. So John made up some excuse, saying he had to watch his nephew or something. But he texted Tyler afterward, saying, wow, amazing match, what did you think? He got no response.

It was thirteen days before payday. "I think I'll be able to get myself out of the woods soon," he told people. The secret? "Not eating, not drinking, smoking less, not going out and cooking at home. It's a very miserable life, but I know how to do it." That was the plan, but it wasn't really going to happen. He spent most of the week with people buying him beers, sinking into a pleasant summery haze, out all night, a little green in the morning, feeling all thin and empty.

JASON FILLED AN awkward place in Edward's absence, and John was studiously pretending Jason hadn't made a confession of affection. They'd get over it, right? Time would pass! One night Jason and Fred and John went out. And Jason was talking to some stranger, and something about Edward's boyfriend came up, and John said, oh, wait, you know Aric? And this guy was like, oh yeah, Aric, he's doing this and that now.

Aric! That was his name. I had no idea that Edward's boyfriend was three-dimensional, John thought. People never brought him up. Edward never talked about him. John had always thought he was kind of imaginary. He'd seen his Facebook and found him on the Internet's burgeoning if simplistic repository of all searchable public images. So he'd seen the face but nothing else. He's the enemy of my life and I don't even know who he is, he thought.

WHEN NEW BUILDINGS would create public outdoor seating, or the City itself would put benches in parks, this furniture would be designed in such a manner that its structural elements would prevent people from using it for reclining fully. These elements were not such radical interventions that one couldn't sit down and rest or eat a lunch! But they would include crosspieces and arm-rests or what have you, or even more obvious decorative elements, regularly repeating, dramatic and intrusive enough. The value then was that it was more important that benches weren't taken up with sleeping people than that people without homes might come across some-where in public to sleep.

GROWING UP, JOHN had only really been to one beach. His family never went to the beaches near them but drove through the City and out to its beaches beyond that, where rich people lived. That's when the family was doing very well. They were rich, or close to it, before his parents died and all the money went with them. They had a beautiful big house.

So his beach experience was specific. You would go there, you read, you relaxed. The adults would have a few beers.

Then the remaining family didn't do that anymore.

Toward the end of his vacation week, John was invited out to a beach house by some older friends—guys who were coupled up, who didn't go out to the bars much.

The house was on a long skinny sand bar, basically, that ran much of the length of the seaside of a larger island, which itself jutted out into the ocean from the City. Sally was coming too. John left the train station on Friday at nine a.m., and he got in a little bus shuttle from the train station to the ferry. All of the passengers were men. He thought they were mostly old, and not attractive.

Then he got to the boat to the island—actually, two boats, for two separate towns. One line was for slick-haired young people, mostly men, and the other was for older people and women. The other ferry full of pretty guys was not going where he was going, and he was with the older people who were not wearing nice clothes. And so he got on his boat and was a little sad. The boats left right next to each other from a little harbor, and as they went out in the bay on their twenty-minute voyage, they got farther and farther apart. John was calculating the walking time between the boat's destinations in his head. He pegged it at about thirty minutes. He sat in the back of the boat, out in the air, as they skimmed out over the shallow blue bay.

His hosts, the couple, greeted him at the dock. It was just a little walk to their house. There were no cars on the island; it was too small. The house was a two-story wood shingle thing, little, with lots of glass, set down in a little forest. It cost twenty-six thousand dollars to rent for the season, which was fairly cheap for the island. In the house they were fussing, cleaning the pool, weeding around the tomatoes in the backyard, talking about the brunch menu for the next day. John had a few beers. One of the hosts, David, took John on a bike ride, down the barrier island but away from the town with all the nicely dressed men, on a hilly, twisty little wooden boardwalk through a dark and green and gray forest, and John fell off his bike and David kept riding, off into the curvy woods. They were barefoot, and John was a little bloody when he got back to the house.

They decided to take naps and then go over to the town where the rich and pretty people lived. At five thirty, John woke up his hosts; they were snoring on the couches.

They set out and walked and walked; the roads were thin at first, maybe four or five feet wide, and made of brown wood. Then they stopped, suddenly, in a little field of tall grass, phragmites. In some parts of the world, the tall thin reed was used for roofing. Here it just blew in the wind and at the top it gave off seeds, like a wheaty flower, and its rhizomes branched and crawled down to the bay and drowned. Beyond the reeds, there was a holly forest and some scrubby pines—originally from all the way around the world—and bramble and impassable areas, hiding stomped-down hutches where deer slept in the day.

John saw some good-looking guys, and he said hey, and they said hey.

They twisted and turned through the forest in the sand, and they came to the next town, where the houses were bigger and the people were younger. It was well still light when they showed up at the center of town, which was built around a little harbor. There was a bar there called the Blue Whale, and John thought everyone there was very old. He had a gimlet. And then he thought maybe the guys weren't so bad. Maybe, he thought, he would have sex with an old guy, something he never did.

"Never talk to anyone with a backpack," David said. "A person with a backpack is a loser." The presence of luggage meant, he explained, that they didn't have a house on the island and were merely passing through. There were all these rules that his hosts imparted to him, about who to talk to and who not to talk to and why. There were more gimlets. And then younger guys showed up. But the long summer day had ended and it was almost dark, and then they all went to the grocery store and got steaks and shrimp, and then it was dark and they were walking, stumbling really, all the way back through the winding woods. It was ten at night and darker than it ever

was in the City, and everyone was starving but the dinner was fantastic.

So what am I going to do tonight? John asked. One of his hosts threw a copy of a glossy little magazine at him. It had event listings. The DJ for the party at the club in town that night was Daniel, of DList infamy, who threw parties in the City that John went to all the time. It was to be an "underwear party."

David gave John some advice. Look, John, here's the deal, he said. Everyone comes here every weekend, starting in May. Now we're a few months in. Everyone from the rich town is going to come over here; this is the night they decide, hey, let's go over to the poor dumpy town for once.

A little after midnight, John set out alone for the club. It was very near the house. This bar was sort of perched on stilts and up a steep wooden stair. There was a line outside, and at the front of the line, each person was stripping and throwing his clothes in garbage bags.

When you stripped down to your underwear, you didn't have any pockets. So John took six cigarettes, some cash and a lighter and stuffed them in his underwear and entered the bar.

That was when he realized that he thought every party should be an underwear party. It gave him this feeling of:

This is who I am. But also: This is what I've got. He felt like the bodies were a kind of currency, which heightened tension between people, but at the same time it fostered a sense of relaxation, with all that mystery eliminated.

Nearly everyone there also lived in the City. And yet John recognized nobody. He felt anonymous, like they were all in a place none of them would ever come to again, and none of them would ever see each other again.

There was some other dark hidden room in the bar. From its entrance, people would emerge looking all insane and disordered. He went to look. It was dark. There were like two or three dozen people in there. And so John went in and then someone was touching him, but John couldn't really tell who it was. And then, after a while, John said to this fellow, do you want to go out for a cigarette? The guy was a flight attendant who lived in a trashy city down in the south of the country. That reminded John of a famous character from when he was young who was called Patient Zero. Just as a woman popularly called Typhoid Mary once was said to have spread typhus while being healthy herself, there was also a man named Gaëtan Dugas some eighty years later. He was a flight attendant who, some said, spread the most recent contagion between men in different cities on his travels, and so he was called Patient Zero:

He was, supposedly, mythically, the patient before all the other patients.

Anyway, this flight attendant was not attractive to him at all, out in the mild light of the balconies on the edge of the bar, so John decided to shake him off. This was a party where the cutest ones were at the fringes, laughing with their friends.

But then, peeking into the back room, he saw this one cute guy who was getting a blow job. He and John made eye contact.

The guy ditched who he was with and came over to John.

After their brief and rote exchange, the guy popped up and said, I'm Taylor. Do you want to go to the bathroom and wash up?

And John said, so you're Taylor?

And Taylor was like, yeah, like Taylor Swift—which was the name of a singer.

And John was like, so I would totally take down your number but obviously I don't have my phone on me, since it's an underwear party.

Wait, you're leaving? Taylor said.

And John said, uh, well yeah, what else is there to do?

So you came, you saw and you conquered and now you just take off, Taylor said.

Well, I feel like my work here is done, John said.

Whatever, Taylor said.

Well, I would take down your number, you're cute and all, John said.

That's cool, Taylor said. I'll see you on the beach.

What an idiot, John thought.

The next morning, Sally arrived in town, in time for brunch. Some muscly guys came over too. John found one annoying, the other less annoying. Also he was overtired and hungover, and he thought he was going to throw up the whole time.

They went to the beach. David made John take a walk with him toward the rich town. There they were all arrayed in Speedos. John was wearing a tiny black swimsuit and felt uncomfortable. Not that he would swim, because he didn't know how. There was a nude guy on the beach. "David, don't look," John said. It was Taylor.

"There's no way he saw us," John said.

"Yes, he did," David said. "And tonight he's going to yell at you and call you a bitch for not waving."

They went home. They took naps. It was so calm.

The only problem, John thought, was that the taste for adventure, or chaos, or something worse was in his mouth now.

That night they all went to the rich town again. John

was trying to focus on the path, to learn it. But he was more lost than ever and felt so blind.

The dance club was having an electrical fire, so they went next door to the little club where ordinarily no one would be. John went to get a drink—he went to get everyone a drink—and there was a good-looking guy on the way to the bar, one that he'd seen the night before. "Yo, what's up," the hot guy said.

"Nothing, what's going on?" John said.

"You're hot," the guy said. They chatted for a minute and then they started kissing at the bar for like five minutes. So John came back without drinks.

"You will notice in the next twenty minutes or so that this place will empty out," David said. Whatever, John thought. In twenty minutes the whole place was empty.

And then: "Everyone goes to dinner at this time," David said. It was ten p.m. on the dot.

They went for a long creepy walk in the dark, through the black-and-green maze of the town, the trees shuddering in the wind off the ocean. All you could hear was silverware clanging in the dark, dishes being put down, people laughing over dinner. You could see little glimpses of warm lit windows and, inside, happy faces.

Finally they got home and had a late dinner of steak—they were all starving.

Everyone was reading and relaxing, but John was pounding beers. He'd resolved that he'd try the nearest bar again, especially so he wouldn't have to walk so far.

But the bar, when he got there, seemed terrible. So he set out on the beach, sensibly, aiming for the other town. Finally he found the path: He came across three guys at the edge of town buckling up their pants. He walked and walked and walked and couldn't find anything, no houses, just sand and trees, but then he saw an enormous flag attached to a house and figured out where he was. So he marched up the beach and was knocked straight back. A small part of the beach was roped off for the nesting of an endangered bird species. The piping plovers! They weren't very interesting birds at all: Tiny, they'd run along the ocean in the day, and at night, who knows. There were lots of animals like this that wouldn't exist for much longer.

At the top of the wooden stairs leading up from the beach, he could hear the music carried on the wind from downtown. He followed it. The bars were packed.

He circulated; he smoked a few cigarettes. Some guy started talking to him—from his neighborhood too, where John knew him from the bars. John told him it was his first time here.

"Oh, honey," the guy said. "So who did you sleep with last night?"

"Oh, I dunno, some guy named Taylor," John said.

"Of course," the guy said, "he's a slut."

"Is he?" John said.

"He's a really friendly slut though," the guy said.

Then across the room, John saw this other guy who had been his mortal enemy in school. It totally ruined his spirit. The guy was with a big group. The evening began to be about weaving through the crowd, trying to avoid the guy from high school. Eventually John went running outside and ran right into Taylor.

"You're a bitch," Taylor said.

"What!" John said.

"You didn't wave to me on the beach," Taylor said.

"How did you even see me?" John said.

"Anyway, this is my friend Dennis," Taylor said.

Dennis looked like a cartoon character. He was cute. And then they had some guy who John thought was really gross-looking with them. So John hung out with them and Dennis kept shooting him meaningful looks. Like crazy. And then Taylor left for a minute and John and Dennis started kissing. And Taylor came back, and John wondered if he'd be mad. But then Taylor and John started making out.

"Let's go back to your house and go in the tub," Dennis said.

"Okay, bitch, let me buy one more drink," Taylor said.

"Why would you buy one more drink when we're about to leave?" John said.

"Obviously because, like, we'll take it with us," Taylor said.

So they went stumbling down the creaky boardwalks in the wind to their house, and they banged through the house and went out into the backyard to the hot tub. The tub wasn't really working; it kept overflowing and shutting off. John looked around. The house was kind of shitty; it was one-story, but it had been just cavernous until random little walls had been put up to create seedy little rooms.

"Fuck, why isn't this thing working!" Taylor said.

Finally it did, and then John and Taylor and Dennis were going at it in the tub.

But their friend that John didn't like was there too. And he kept touching John, and John kept shaking him off. Then the tub stopped working again.

"Fuck it, I'm going home," Dennis said.

It was maybe three or four in the morning. The owner of the house showed up. He kept talking about how much he loved political conservatives. He got in the tub. Everyone kind of sat there and then the night was ending and the owner started giving directions.

"First of all, John, you're beautiful and wonderful, so you'll be with us tomorrow," he said. "What's going to happen here is, you will sleep with Taylor tonight for the second night in a row. You guys will sleep on the couch out on the living room. Tomorrow we're going to a party at eleven a.m., and I'll have a lot of coke for us. Then we have another party at four thirty. I'm so sorry, John, I can't offer you any blow tonight."

The orders went on. Taylor seemed anxious. Clearly he wanted to be accommodating and polite to the owner, since after all he stayed there at his discretion, solely because he was good-looking.

They got away, eventually. The night turned blue. John said, "Let's go somewhere."

"Where do you want to go?" Taylor said. "Everything's closed."

"Can't we just go to the Meat Rack or something?" John said.

"It's not really good at this time," Taylor said.

"Alright, I mean, well, you're the expert," John said.

"Can we just have sex?" Taylor said.

Then they had sex on the couch. They made a lot of noise. The whole house probably heard.

"Okay, I'm going," John said. It wasn't night anymore.

"Why aren't you staying?" Taylor said.

"Good seeing you," John said.

John was feeling guilty at this point. He took Taylor's phone number. He'd stayed up all night, away from his hosts, ending up at some coke party. And they'd never used a condom during sex, the whole time. He felt disgusting and panicked.

And earlier John had asked Taylor, as a joke, "Who have you done today?" And Taylor was like, "Oh, some guy I just picked up off the street." And John had asked, how was the rest of last night, after I left you? And Taylor was like, "Oh my God, it got so crazy!" John was trashed. He'd been trashed for days now. What he thought was the worst was that he realized this was the kind of fun he'd set out looking for: boys, drugs, excitement, booze. The hunt and its success. He was out of the town by then and walking through the woods and the birds were chirping, it was disgusting out, and suddenly again there was the guy from his neighborhood. "Oh hi!" John said. And the guy could barely get it together to speak either.

It was a common nightmare in which you did something you never wanted to do, but then you woke up, and you hadn't actually done it, and you were relieved. But when it wasn't a nightmare, there was no relief.

The night was getting lemony and pale; it was almost-day night. Like there was the light of two moons or something. There were guys stumbling out of bushes. It really was a maze. Finally John stopped a man and asked how to get home, and the man said, "Just follow me."

They walked and walked. "My sister just died," the stranger said.

He got home at seven thirty a.m. He sneaked in the house, all burned out inside. No one heard him.

He woke up at almost one in the afternoon. He came downstairs.

"Are we going to the beach?" John said.

"No, we've all been to the beach. We're going back to the City in forty-five minutes," one of his hosts said.

Instead of showering, he went out in the backyard and got in the little long black-lined pool. He felt depleted. Sally was holding him up so that he wouldn't drown. Disaster. He was idly kicking, too tense to drift, too anxious to listen, sad as he could be.

II.

In a very old and still popular history book, there was a story about a man who said he talked to God. When he was no longer a boy, he confided in his family that he heard voices. So obviously he became employed as a prophet and as a military general. And when he was old and famous, the people said to him, "This system we have just isn't working out. We're ready for something new, and we would like you to tell us who should be our king."

But their prophet said, "That's a terrible idea. If you have a king, he'll conscript your children. He'll make you do his field-work. He'll have your daughters make his bread. He'll take the best things you grow for his people. And then he'll take ten percent of your vegetables and grains and the wine that you make—and that's just for his servants! He'll take ten percent of your sheep. Basically, you'll all be his slaves. Eventually, you'll be sorry, and you'll have no one to blame but yourselves."

But from time immemorial—and this was indeed a very long time ago—people have wanted someone in charge. They knew that the person in charge would be terrible, because only a hardheaded and rash and possibly psychopathic person was good at defending a country. Countries wanted to expand, always, and fortify their borders; their leaders personified that need to ooze over maps, over dusty hills, creeping along rivers, seizing and insulating.

So this prophet consulted with the voices he heard, and the voices said, go on, go ahead! Give them a king then, if they want one so bad.

For thousands of years after, the people were always plagued by kings. The kings came in all varieties and titles, but they all shared the love of territory and capital, the love of oozing and taking and fortification and celebrity.

The kings changed their methods over time. Later, the kings were only sometimes military or countrywide kings. All over the world, there were kings that had mere hundreds or maybe thousands or tens of thousands of subjects, but most often they were corporate kings. They let people farm the land for them and keep some profit. Or they bought up all the jobs in a town, as giant merchants, and then owned many of the workers in town for their kingdom. Or they owned all the land and so everyone paid them rent.

You were a king if no one could compete with you, and if no subject could easily leave your kingdom—the less porous your kingdom, the greater your kingship.

While many countries were subject to kings, the City itself was so compressed, so vertical, so tall with kings, that in fact the citizens had more freedom from local kings. There were so many opportunities to become a king, and some were immensely successful and some were less so. Mostly the kings were too busy with each other, oozing and creeping their kingdoms in perpetual alliances and skirmishes. So the people could, usually, hop from kingdom to kingdom.

What had changed over those thousands of years were a few things. Many things did not change; always, there was land and royal matchmaking and trade. Of course there were always more people who wanted to and had to pay for things. And then, in concert with the growing number of people, they invented new kinds of things that people had to pay for. For instance, once you "paid" for water by getting together with others and digging a well; then you all owned it. Now people who lived in cities did not have that equity from their labor; instead they paid for water to be delivered continuously to their homes. It was always on.

There were other things—games and fashions and trinkets and entertainments—that were merely advanced evolutions of age-old markets, from the necessary to the enjoyable to the frivolous. There was, for instance, medical treatment, which at this time hovered confusingly between being a right and being an unobtainable luxury.

THE CITY WAS all soft and steamy and delirious. Tree roots pushed up against slab, patient, growing every day. Down in the old former swamps of the City, where the hard schist broke up or dove down, the roots roamed wet and free, and pushed up because they could, and pushed down through garbage and broken rock and landfill. The old buildings sagged. In the bathrooms a tile would crack, and then another. One day a window wouldn't quite close square. The old hills from the west side pushed down what was once an old former soggy cove. The rocks and burned buildings and gravel that filled in the swamps and unevenness of the east side, that mass was all compressed and thick now from decades of pressure, held together by webs of pipes and wires and roots and time. Little dirty streams appeared in the subway tunnels. Hundreds of pumps moved millions of gallons of water from the boreholes into tunnels built for wastewater, and then pumped it back into the sea. The sea shoved the water back. The more of the City there was, the heavier it got. All things settled, but not without constant tension, and often, unnoticed, a thing would quietly break. The great heap of structures made allowances one after another after the next for as long as it could.

JOHN BOUGHT A loaf of bread for dinner and was asleep by the stroke of nine.

He'd been texting Taylor back and forth, like dozens of times.

"I have nothing to hide," Taylor had texted.

"You have my number," Taylor had texted.

John awoke to the humming of his phone, another text from Taylor. "Don't worry," Taylor texted.

Then it was three a.m. and he couldn't go back to sleep in the dark and hot and quiet, and he stayed up and watched some terrible movie on the TV.

IN JOHN'S MAIL there came a bank statement, for the period of June 22 to July 21.

His checking had 0.41 dollars. His savings had 0.85 dollars. His delinquent loan payments were 1,496.04 dollars. His Checking Plus Credit Line minimum payment due was 43.36 dollars. His annual percentage rate for interest on that was 15.25 percent. The amount of money subtracted from his bank account in that period was 2,581.07 dollars. But the amount of money he'd put into his bank account in that period was 2,272.72 dollars.

On June 14, he'd made a debit card purchase at a fast food hamburger place in the amount of 4.74 dollars.

JASON HAD BEEN to the same beach town once as well, he said.

"Oh my God, one time I went through the forest and I like totally hit my head into one of those branches and nearly lost my eye and I had to wear an eye patch for weeks but so then I went back home and I realized my wallet was totally gone and my eye was hanging out of my socket so I went back out there and I knew exactly where it was and I was walking in the dark and I saw these two guys and I'm like, you have my wallet, don't you, and these guys were making out and they were like, no, we don't, and I'm like, yes, you do, and the one guy says to the other, c'mon give it back, and then they gave me my wallet back. It was pretty amazing."

AT THIS TIME, people still weren't entirely sure of their origins. Most people throughout time had kept records, but they were always such confusing records. First, the records were so myopic and self-centered that they didn't make much sense to people who came later, with off-hand references that would make no sense after twenty or two hundred or two thousand years. And then, people made records that were created physically in an impermanent and shortsighted fashion, and many of these had deteriorated, or burned, or the machinery that could read them no longer existed. And then, if a history survived that, often it happened that these documents had been translated so many times, into language after language, that they stopped being intelligible.

And there weren't many very early records at all. Many human scientists were convinced—by means of records of fossils, and because it had been noticed that animals that were isolated for long periods of time became distinct and novel—that people had been alive for a long time and that they might very well have slowly sprung from an animal, or a group of animals, quite some time previous.

But many other people did not believe this. Mainly theistic groups argued that schools should not be allowed to teach, as a theory, that humans might be descended from other animals.

Groups cohered around almost every idea—what people could do with their bodies, what people could do with the bodies of other people. People even disagreed at this time if the seas on the planet would rise and drown all the cities.

Because this sort of organizing was divisive, it was therefore important for social selection. Most people self-selected their friends based on shared ideas and behaviors. Groups of friends or lovers tended to agree, largely or mostly, on ideas about politics, or how to live, or about whether we might have come from animals, or about morals in general.

This tendency to self-select one's social sphere, to gather around agreement, caused many cities to exhibit prevailing sets of ethics and moral codes. The City, for instance, while populated by diverse viewpoints, on the whole tended toward hedonism, and toward the legality and practice of abortion, which was a currently legal but not entirely popular medical procedure that terminated pregnancies. The City's inhabitants tended away from religious practice overall, or at least tended toward diverse and conflicting religions, and so therefore knew that a tolerance for other viewpoints was in their self-interest. The City, in comparison to much of the rest of the country, tended toward appreciating difference rather than punishing it. And as a reflection of this, the Mayor, particularly for an extremely wealthy person, was fairly "open-minded," believing firmly as a principle that people should have broad rights of behavior, even while believing at the same time that the government should and could limit behaviors. This was a somewhat unusual position, in the larger scheme of beliefs, and a mildly unusual position for people of his class.

Tendency toward this set of beliefs about freedom was more pronounced among people who had moved to the City from other parts of the country. And then a significant number of people in the City—about three million—were immigrants from other countries, and, very broadly, they tended to be more "conservative" and more religious. But these immigrants—again, most broadly—tended also not to mix socially with the people who'd come to the City from other parts of the country. The poorer of these immigrants encountered other kinds of residents at places of employment, largely, where immigrants often worked in service positions, at delis, restaurants, retail stores and in people's homes, cleaning and/or taking care of their children. These positions were low paid, most often; sometimes they were "off the books," which meant that the jobs were not reported to the government.

These were people who would not ordinarily associate with each other.

And then as all these different people assimilated into the City, they tended to see that they benefited from tolerance of difference because, as they may have been surprised to find, they were listed among "the different."

Most people, for instance, wanted to live near people like them, and so the City was composed of some neighborhoods that were diverse and some neighborhoods that were somewhat uniform. Some of these more uniform neighborhoods even had a dominant minority language. But then as people born to immigrants grew up in those little villages, they felt, quite rightly, that the City as a whole was theirs too, and they often moved themselves into neighborhoods of more diversity.

In the end, some people were relatively obsessed with where people came from, and some people didn't really care at all, while others were figuring out where people were going in the immediate future, largely by moving and amassing capital.

It was the very near future they were interested in most of all; the human lifespan was not that long, and while some people captured capital for the benefit of their children and their children's children, the influence that came with having capital was not particularly well exercised by the dead.

JOHN SPENT A nice enough Sunday at a party on Fifth Avenue with Fred, and this party was thrown apparently by some nuclear physicists who John and Fred agreed made the kid with craniodiaphyseal dysplasia from *Mask* look like Brad Pitt. That was a rude way for them to say that these guys weren't attractive. But it was a fun party and they were all weird and losers and it was great. It was all hot out and they were outside. And so John texted his friends to come over too—and Edward showed up, having tagged along with them.

John was so mad, he wouldn't look at him.

After that he didn't make contact with Edward for a week. No emails, nothing. I hate him right now, John told everyone.

Edward pushes me off but he comes running back, John thought. So. He's really cute, he's really charming, and also he's a mess. He's looking for work. He doesn't even have a bank account. But then John would tabulate the not-bad things: He had a life that was interesting, and John liked that. One thing he always worried about was that he would be smothered in a relationship, and he didn't think Edward would do that. But Edward had his boyfriend, or whatever— did he?—and his weird situation, and John wasn't going to deal with that. Edward needed to say: I broke up with my boyfriend. I want you—I want to be with you. And I'll have my own place in the City. Those three things had to happen. Instead Edward's message to him was simply: You blow me away like no one ever has before. And to that, John thought, well, whatever: not at all good enough.

JOHN TEXTED TYLER Flowers: Do you wanna go to the park? Texts were weird; they were intrusive in a way that Internet chatting wasn't. Your mobile phone would beep or chirp; you didn't have to be at the computer, waiting to be entertained. You didn't access it at your leisure. Among forms of communication, it was the imperative mode. You: Answer me now. And Tyler responded, hmm I'm really busy this week, sorry.

So is he just done with me? John asked Fred. No, Fred said, he's actually busy, he has a fuck buddy from out of town in town. Alright, makes sense, John thought, I won't take it personally.

JOHN WENT BACK to work and Friday rolled around, and he met some guy named Chris, who worked at a fancy magazine. They met at a party. And Chris later messaged John on Manhunt, and as he did, he "unlocked" all his pictures stored online, thereby making them visible to John. John did have public pictures of his face on Manhunt that week, so this "unlocking" was Chris's way of saying, "Hey! We know each other!" So they chatted a little. Chris wrote, I was going to ask for your real email. Chris said that he was having a party, and that John should come.

So of course John IM'd Fred, and said, hey, this guy

Chris is having a party, do you want to go? And Fred wrote back, actually I am already planning to attend that party—and I'm going with Tyler Flowers.

John immediately emailed Tyler, to prevent a one-sided unexpected run-in. Oh my God, this week has been so crazy! he wrote. I can't believe we haven't met up! Anyway, I'm going to this party tonight, if you want to go, I'm really on the fence, but if you were going . . . or we can do next week!

And Tyler wrote back, oh, you mean Chris's party? And John wrote back, oh yes, that's so weird-funny, why don't you meet me there, I'm meeting Jason, we're meeting at Nowhere Bar at ten thirty and then taking the train, join us there! And Tyler said he would.

So the evening came on and John called Tyler to check in, and Tyler said, can't we just take a cab? A cab would cost maybe twenty dollars. So John was firm: I'll see you at Nowhere. It'd be ridiculous for you to be in the same neighborhood and not travel with me, so I'll see you at Nowhere. Tyler relented.

So they all show up at Nowhere Bar. Basically all you could see in there was Jason's bald head gleaming. You totally had to beg me to come here, Tyler Flowers said.

I insisted, I did not beg you, John said.

You had to beg me! Oh, I'm just kidding! Tyler said.

John was having fun with Jason, even though Tyler was in this weird hostile mood. Tyler had three beers. It was finally late enough to wait to go to the party, and they walked to the R train.

"I can't believe we're taking the fucking train, this is fucking bullshit," Tyler said.

"Just take the train, don't worry about it," John said.

"I should have brought the *New Yorker*," Tyler said.

"You can go buy one if you don't want to talk to us!" John said.

"No, I'm sorry, I didn't mean it, I just need a drink, guys, I just need a drink," Tyler said.

Jason and John kept looking at each other, like, what is this.

They got on the train; it stopped just a few stops later and wouldn't go any farther. We can just transfer trains, John said. So they went and waited on the platform but it didn't come.

"We're just taking a fucking cab!" Tyler said, and stormed out.

They ran after him. He had gotten a cab.

"I don't even know why we're going over there!" Tyler said. "Whenever you go, it's a disaster!"

Why had he chased this horrible guy? John wondered. The cab ride was fourteen dollars. John had something like two dollars. "What is this? You can pay with a card now? How do I do this?" Tyler asked.

He was staring at the keypad installed in the back of the driver's seat. John hit all the buttons so Tyler could pay with a credit card. Tyler keyed in one dollar for a tip. And John said, oh, I have a couple dollars for a tip! And Jason said, yeah, I have a five here for the cabbie.

"No," Tyler said. "One dollar is okay."

They got out of the cab, and they asked, why one dollar?

"Everyone knows that," Tyler said. "If it's anything less than eighteen dollars, you tip one dollar."

"Is this some rule from the nineties?" John asked.

"No, everyone knows that, and why should I give him more when it's his job to drive?"

"Maybe because we brought him way out here?" John said.

"Whatever, I just need a drink, I'm sorry," Tyler said.

The apartment wasn't that big and was kind of crowded and eventually John was out smoking on this fire escape. He climbed back in and Tyler was there. I wondered where you were, I'm so much more relaxed, I don't know why I was so worked up, I just needed a drink in me, Tyler said.

"Oh okay, no problem," John said. So they all re-formed into a group and took off. They ended up at a terrible bar in the neighborhood. There were like six people in there. Fred, Jason, Tyler—and this random terrible guy, who was totally evil. They were outside smoking and John said, I'm experimenting with a new tennis grip, semi-western.

"What else would you use?" this guy said.

"Uh, what?" John said. And the guy started going off about how there's really only one way to play tennis, there's only one way to hold a racket, that kind of thing.

"Well, I grew up playing with a bamboo stick and crumpled up newspapers," John said. He went kind of crazy on him.

They took the subway back, Jason and Tyler and John. Tyler and John were on the verge of making out. Finally! John thought. And then he saw: Jason, sitting across from them on the train, basically with tears in his eyes, watching them. And Tyler was ready to go, his stop was coming up. And John thought: Fine. Guess I won't get off the train with him right here in front of Jason. So good-bye, John said, see you later!

And when John got home, he sent a text message to Tyler, just: "Heyyyy." And Tyler wrote back, "Ha ha!" And John wrote back, "What's up?" And Tyler wrote back, "Not much!" And John wrote back, "You were totally better after you got that drink!" And then Tyler didn't write back.

But the next morning he did write back. "Sorry, I fell asleep, sorry I was such a bitch."

What a complicated deal to close! Finally John wrote Tyler on Facebook and was like, when are you leaving town for that trip, let's have a drink or a cheap dinner, just you and me. And Tyler wrote back, sounds like fun, Friday or Saturday. I don't even like him, John thought.

THE IMMEDIATELY PREVIOUS mayor told the City to be afraid if they did not reelect the Mayor. This previous mayor now made all his money from speaking engagements, providing fairly useless advice to corporations and other cities on their safety, and also lobbying for companies that polluted the planet. If they did not reelect the Mayor, he said, they would be afraid to go outside and walk the streets. "You know exactly what I'm talking about," he told a room of older people. "This city could easily be taken back in a very different direction." He meant muggings, and poor people running wild against rich people, and who knows what, it was a vague threat, but he meant something.

FRED SENT JOHN an old Internet chat transcript—from the summer two years prior. At the time, Fred had been actually kind of dating Tyler.

fred: who are you fucking these days?

   sorry. that was a vulgar question

   i need ac

john: a hipster, a blogger and a park slope boy

fred: how's the park slope boy?

john: he's the worst of the batch. so thank god he's far away

fred: i'm also doing this hot hipster, but he's leaving for

   europe in a week or two

john: i can't maintain any relationship

fred: yeah. these aren't relationships

john: they all fall apart, somehow

   i know, but i long for lost fuck buddies

fred: yeah. all i want now is just somebody i wanna fuck

   more than three times

JASON SAW A guy on the train, going home. They made a lot of eye contact. They got off at the same stop—Jason was walking a bit behind him. Well, he kind of followed him, but in a way he hoped wasn't stalkery. And then the guy met someone at the end of the block so Jason turned about and aborted mission.

When he got home, he went on the Internet, and he put up a "Missed Connections" post on Craigslist. That was a bulletin board for people who'd encountered each other but had no other way of identifying or reaching the other person. It was surprisingly effective for this kind of reunion. His post read something like: You were wearing a salmon cardigan and got off the train. And an hour after he posted it, the guy sent an email through the system and included his picture. His note said: I think you mean me? So they went for a drink, but a drink in the neighborhood, so it was convenient to go straight back home, which they totally did.

Then a few nights later, he texted Jason late, late, late at night. His text just said: "Sup." Jason didn't bother texting back.

CHAD AND DIEGO decided they wanted to move in together. Chad's roommate was leaving, for one thing, and so it was a convergence of desire and logistics and economics. Way back in spring they had begun thinking about this and then Chad's lease ended at the end of July. A friend of a friend of a friend of Chad's was a sort of fancy but no-fee real estate broker, so she showed him the cheapest of her listings. They saw an apartment way out from the center of the City, and they really liked it—a two-bedroom for 1,200 dollars. It was on a two-block street called Regent Place. Not only was Regent Place in the running for the most unsafe place in the City, according to the random chatter Chad saw on the

Internet, but the apartment next door to the one they'd been shown was the site of a major drug bust three months before. They regrouped. They wanted to be on the train that went to the neighborhoods where all their friends lived. It was important to John that Chad be accessible via subway.

Chad had been paying 650 dollars before, and Diego maybe slightly less. They were looking for one-bedrooms for 1,400 dollars or so, and found one for 1,350. So it worked out, they thought. Though it would take a while to get in. They had to stay at Chad's parents for two weeks while it all worked out. Chad's mom had just gotten a promotion at work. She was the only person that Chad knew who'd had any kind of career advancement that year. They were even renovating their bathrooms.

And Chad was getting 500 dollars a month in piecework from John's company. Chad had made enough money in the spring that he didn't really have to make much money this summer. Also he'd been drinking less!

The tutoring business was better than ever. When Chad didn't have other income, he just picked up more clients. The agency was always contacting Chad with more students than he could manage. For spring he'd maybe had five students a week, at 100 dollars per student per week. But this work also kept Chad from reaching out to do better things. It kept him comfortable and fed, and he didn't spend a lot of money, and he wore the same sweater all the time. Plus Chad had no debt because his school had no student loans. And Diego made like 40,000 dollars a year and had just a little debt, but they also lived really cheaply. Chad had about 15,000 dollars in savings. He spent only 1,500 to 2,000 a month. He was on a "family plan" for his cell phone, but his family never paid for anything else. Back when he'd had a real office job, and made 25,000 dollars a year, well, he thought that in that case, one should be paying 600 dollars a month in rent, not 1,100 dollars.

Chad was becoming Joni Mitchell–friends with Edward. That meant he'd IM with Edward and they'd talk about Joni Mitchell. Also, Edward wanted to talk about John a lot.

Chad's mom loved John. Chad was talking to her about John shortly after he moved in for his temporary stay. John had come and stayed for a few days too, and then gone back home. They thought John had issues with money that kept him from improving his life. They thought there could be little sacrifices he could make. But it was so much all tied in with his family and feeling very bad about money. He actually hated money, they thought. He wanted it to leave him as soon as it possibly could. Chad thought John saw the very idea of money as being all wrapped up in the death of his father. But Chad's mom said that she thought that John just believed that he didn't deserve any security.

It was unthinkable to Chad that John had never been in therapy, which was a process of recalibration during which you talked with someone to discover things about yourself. And Chad thought John still blamed himself for his father's death. And he thought John was happy in some ways but not in others, and that father surrogates would always be disappointing to him. Father surrogates actually couldn't be there for you, not in a meaningful way. If they were your boss, for instance, they would leave at the end of the day.

While John was there with Chad's parents, John had finally told·Chad the whole story straight out. John believed that if something happened, you just had to move on. Not dealing with finances was a way of putting off dealing with all of these things. It was a way of putting off adulthood. Being an adult might be stressful, but so was being a child, and being childlike. That anxiety, and its constant presence, was what kept John on the run. Thomas quitting meant more than he could say. It confirmed his sense that people would always abandon you.

They talked about having sex without condoms—and

Chad had done this too, in the past—but Chad would plead with John: Please don't do that again. He couldn't bear the idea of something so bad, and so unnecessary, happening to John. Chad worried about John all the time but also he tried not to.

THE STRETCH OF living with Chad's parents dragged on all through hot August. The apartment wasn't ready. His parents lived way, way out, and he would take the train to the end of the line, out past the airport, and then they'd come and pick him up. One night it was about ten and there were about six people in the train car. He was sitting on a bank of four chairs, and his calf was up touching another chair, his whole leg extended. And the train stopped at an aboveground station and he heard some voice. It said, "Get off the train." And this big guy in street clothes came over and held up a badge. "Get off the train," he said, holding the doors open. This was in the first car, so he looked at the conductor, and the conductor said, yeah, it's okay.

"How many seats did you pay for?" the man asked.

Chad thought about it. Trick question, he thought. I paid for a ride, not a seat.

"You had your foot on a seat," the man said.

There were many rules for the use of "public" transit, which was not really public; it was a corporation controlled by people proposed by the state and by the Mayor. It was, however, more "public" than it once was; three competing subway systems were consolidated, some sixty years previous, when the two of the systems that were "for-profit" corporations filed for bankruptcy. The City then owned all the subways, and the transit corporation paid the City for their use.

The rules included that no person could engage in any "commercial activity"; no person could take part in any "nontransit uses" of the transit system, including "artistic performances"; there would be no consumption of liquids at all in any "open container"; one might not light a match; one should not gamble; one could not use the trains when one was "impaired" by alcohol or drugs, though what one was supposed to do in that case was unclear; one was forbidden from causing "annoyance, alarm or inconvenience"; one could not place one's foot on any seat; one was not allowed to recline; one could not block escalators or stairways or platforms; and one must not "occupy more than one seat . . . when to do so would interfere or tend to interfere with the operation of the Authority's transit system or the comfort of other passengers."

He gave Chad a fifty-dollar ticket for having his foot on a seat.

Oh, you should absolutely fight it, his friends told him.

EDWARD BROKE UP with his boyfriend, just like that. Perhaps this was something his boyfriend could have seen coming, what with Edward living in the Capital with his parents so much of the time.

Perhaps not. People are surprising, and easily surprised, and also people have always been willfully blind.

Except now Edward was spending more time in town. He would send an email to John that would say, hi, I'm coming up, can I see you? And John would have this ambivalent rush of feelings and in the end? Well. He would.

So Edward and John were talking, at a party, and John had also invited this guy he used to have a crush on too, in a fit of craziness. Originally he was going to invite Tyler Flowers as well. He wanted them all there; he wanted something to happen, to break. Why did he do this, his friends asked, why did he always pile all these people together? "I don't know why!" he said. He did it in part to take Edward at his word. Weren't they not together?

Inevitably John got drunk and mixed up their names.

But then Edward and Jason and John went to take the train home. Edward was going to stay at Jason's, they were pretending. Of course he wasn't. John fell asleep in the subway station with his head in Edward's lap. Some guys walked by and said, "Oh, that looks nice, I wish I could do that," but in a totally hostile, sneering way.

John slept right through it. Then he woke up in time to go home with Edward.

FINALLY IT WAS time for Fred to leave the City. So he had a going-away party.

Edward came in and found John at the bar. This was down in a little neighborhood, not far from the patiently waiting waterfront, clustered under some bridges. Inside it was huge and brown and an absorbing kind of loud, and it was unclear where the party stopped and started; the party itself was a meandering throng of pressed people.

"What do you think is the cheapest beer here? Will you order it for me?" Edward asked.

"I wouldn't be comfortable doing that," John said, quite seriously.

Jason was behind them. He'd just taken a vacation with his ex-lover. That was probably a bad idea. "It was okaaaayyy," he told people, when they asked. He was talking to a glittery-eyed guy, who was very tall and had very intense hair and a big, impressive nose. This guy knew Fred because they'd slept together once, not happily.

"Did you use a C?" this guy asked Jason, aggressive but teasing.

"A connie?" Jason said. He meant a condom.

"Did you come inside him?" the guy asked.

John and Edward went out to smoke and talked about the writer Iris Murdoch. When the glittery guy came out too, John tap-punched him in the stomach. "Those are my abs," the guy said, absently.

It was sticky, and up and to the right was the black looming metal mass of a bridge, so dark and heavy it made all the streets look gray-yellow instead of dark. Cabs and partiers passed on by. It was like being in a secret tiny village hidden inside a big stage set.

"Where does Eleanor Clift live?" Jason asked.

"I'm sure she lives in Chevy," Edward said.

"I never knew she was the sister-in-law of Montgomery Clift!" John said. "I wrote it on my Twitter. This Truman Capote essay I was reading on the train? It was a profile of Elizabeth Taylor, written for *Ladies' Home Journal* in 1967." These were the names of rich people who were all dead.

"Oh my God, link?" Jason said.

"But!" John said. "There's this incredible scene, of course it's like just typical Truman Capote, name-dropping left and right. He's like, so one time we're talking about our mutual friend Montgomery Clift, and he's like, we went to the Gucci store together because Montgomery was depressed, he was like, I'll buy you lunch and I can get you a sweater. So then we went to the Gucci store and he picked out twenty sweaters, and he went outside and threw them in the street and started dancing around them. I kid you not. And the people at Gucci were really good about it. They were like, 'So who are we charging those sweaters to?' and Truman's like, 'Well, I can't afford this!' And he's like, 'Montgomery, we need a credit card.' And he's like, 'This! Face! Is the credit card!' "

"Do you think that might work for me?" Edward said.

"Maaaaybe," Jason said.

"I have no credit cards though. I have my dad's," Edward said.

"It would have been better if he'd charged it to Liz. She's good for it," Jason said.

"That was bananas," John said. "Bye, are you leaving?" A guy had left the bar.

"A friend of ours is flying in from Paris," the guy said, "only for the night. May I please bum a light as well?"

They talked about a party the guy was planning, and how chaotic the City could get.

"This is why I'm moving way out here," the guy said. "I live on Thompson Street."

"Oh boy," John said. That street could be loud.

"So if anyone knows a place opening up . . . ," the guy said.

"You'll be the first to know, I promise," John said with a little too much insincere heartiness.

Things were "booming real estate–wise before September and now—" the guy said.

"And now it's September," John said. "You know what the new theory is about Williamsburg?"

"The new theory?" the guy said.

"That it's settling into middle age. Like people are now moving there—like Trixie and Finn moving there?"

Trixie was John's immediate boss these days, now that Timothy was the overall boss. She was about six years older than him. She and her husband, Finn, were, for now, childless but they did own a cat.

"It's Park Sloping," said someone.

"Exactly," John said. "People are moving from Fort Greene, the nice areas, to Williamsburg now."

"I really like Boerum Hill," the guy said.

"Well, they're all leaving," John said. "Boerum Hill is the new Williamsburg."

"I'm always ahead of the curve," Jason said.

"I'll regentrify Boerum Hill," the guy said. "I'll open a little coffee shop. Well, thanks for the cigarette."

"Alright, guy," John said. "I'll see you Saturday."

"Barbecue. Saturday," the guy said.

He left.

"Oh my God, we just had to talk to Crazy Eyes!" John said.

"He's going to regentrify Brooklyn! Those eyes!" Jason said.

"Oh, he's Crazy Eyes," John said. "It's unbelievable. He's the one who was critical of my semi-western tennis grip. I was like, 'Oh, I'm experimenting with this semi-western tennis grip.' And he was like, 'You don't use that already?' He was like, 'I've been using that for years.'"

Then they talked about Nancy Kerrigan and Tonya Harding for a while.

"Why do I feel this way?" John said. "I can't move."

Later they ended up at Metropolitan, at the bar. Eventually John decided that he was really tired. I have to go home, he said. Jason went to go get his bag, and while he was gone, Edward asked, can I come over? We don't have to, like, do anything, but I'd really like to spend the night with you.

ALL AROUND THE City were signs for the upcoming election. The press was on, and the Mayor was trying to solicit good feelings after making so many people so mad. And everyone expected him to win by a huge margin, so while there was much grumbling, no one minded too much, really, except a little, but also they weren't sure they had any better alternatives. He had a chief competitor who seemed invisible, who seemed pale and unvivid in comparison to the Mayor. No one really felt like he was a character in the story of the City. The challenger just couldn't make himself felt.

The Mayor's third run was a keenly played attack on human nature. The Mayor knew full well that people, who almost always like what they are accustomed to, tended heavily to vote for the candidate already in office. The Mayor had found a way to do something that many people did not want and then, as an encore, to suggest that the people were welcome to reject him if they wished—even while he was spending millions of dollars, just an immense amount of money, in advertising. Advertising was supposed to eat away at any resistance that people felt, and the more times someone saw an ad, supposedly, the more people regarded the product advertised as something they couldn't live without.

SOME OF JOHN'S family had been training for the annual end-of-summer get-together all year. They stayed at a hotel called the Beachcomber. It was super trashy, but also it was right across the highway from the ocean. This beach was as far east as you could go away from the City. The pinnacle of the weekend—for some, at least—was the tennis tournament. John had maybe played only three times all summer. Before he hit the court, he had a few cigarettes and a big glass of gin. He was literally swinging the racket as hard as he could, grunting like a hog.

At the reunion, it was John and his two brothers, his cousins—including his roommate—and his young nephews, Jesse and Julian. All of them had been born in mid-October. Also there was his sister-in-law, Shawn.

Jesse was six years old. John had brought him this book that had been sent to his office. It was called *The Pop-up Book of Sports*.

"Hey, Jesse," John said.

"Hi," Jesse said.

"Jesse, I have a present for you," John said.

"Can I have it now?" Jesse asked.

"No, you have to wait for it later, but aren't you excited?" John said.

"How can you afford it?" Jesse said. "You don't have any money."

"Where did you hear that?" John said.

"From Jake and Shawn," Jesse said. He called his parents by their first names.

John went over to Jake and Shawn.

"Oh, he's just been saying that about everyone these days!" Shawn said.

Shawn was a character. She was actually one of the

three hundred thousand or so people who worked for the City. One day she was wearing a T-shirt that said "I [heart] the City" at work. And this was a time when there was a new shirt, one that said "I [heart] the City more than ever," part of a campaign of improving civic pride. Why aren't you wearing "that" shirt? someone at work asked her. Don't you know? Well, as a matter of fact, Shawn said, I don't heart the City more than ever now.

Then later they were playing football down on the beach, and his brothers got rambunctious and then they got mad, and John called one of them a dick, and they didn't speak for the rest of the trip. Everyone else got into the grudging spirit. Shawn made noise about how cheap John's other brother was. John took the train home and for a good while pretty much nobody in the family talked to each other. In any event John won the tennis tournament for the fifth straight year.

TYLER WROTE JOHN an email. Then he left a voicemail. And on it he was being all cute, yawning, saying, oh, hey, good morning . . . it's Tyler, call me. John thought it was annoying, but Tyler surely thought the opposite. They were going to get together on Monday. So that day John called at like four p.m.

Are we on for later? John asked.

Oh, actually I can't do it, Tyler said. Do you know today's my birthday? He was turning twenty-eight.

No, happy birthday! John said.

Yeah. It's my birthday. So anyway friends are taking me out for dinner. We could do something later this week.

Honestly, this week is really bad for me—

Well then, the week after, whatever!

Or I could do Friday potentially.

Oh okay, Friday.

So what's going on?

Tyler sounded really grumpy.

You're either really hungover or you're really grumpy or maybe it's both.

What?

So then they talked and he started laughing a little. But John was really laboring to make it an actual conversation.

Okay, John, I really have to go, Tyler said.

And John just hung up.

John told this to Chad. It's bullshit, right? Yeah. It's bullshit, Chad said.

John told this to Fred too, overseas. Fred had nothing to do over there, no friends yet, so he was more available than ever. Plus he was "ahead" by five hours. One strategy for dealing with the shape of the earth and the local time of day was stratifying most of the world into "time zones," so it was unified around the world that "morning" would mean sunup, even though this made it just impossible to talk to people when they were in their offices or awake even, sometimes. The time difference in this case was actually helpful—Fred was always up. Fred, I need your advice on this, John said. What's the deal with this?

John, Tyler's really moody, Fred said. I don't think it's worth your time, to be honest. He's really moody and he's entitled in his moodiness.

Friday rolled around. They hadn't talked since Monday, so he texted Tyler: We still on for tonight?

With Chad, John had made a list of five expected excuses, in order of likeliness: sick, it's raining, have dinner with friends, too tired and then: out of town. Then he revised the list: No response at all was a late contender, as the third-most likely.

Twenty minutes later, John got a text: Hey John I have a haircut to get at 9 p.m. tonight. And I have an early start tomorrow. Let's do something quiet, like, next week.

A haircut! Chad lost his mind. That is evil! That is malicious! He was screaming at top volume: "That is fucking bullshit!" But John thought it was pretty funny.

That night, John went out. He went to Metropolitan; he went to Sugarland, where he kissed a few people on the dance floor. He got pretty drunk, and his body felt all gross. He got a text a little after one a.m., from Tyler Flowers. He wrote: "Your girl Alexandra made my night, I owe you one, xo." He'd run into John's coworker Alexandra at a fashion party.

The next day John called Alexandra. I wanted to hear about your night with Tyler Flowers. Tell me the story, he said. Oh, she said. I was leaving the Charlotte Ronson party at like twelve thirty or one with my friend, and as I walked out this guy was shouting my name, Alexandra, Alexandra! And she looked at him and thought, who are you? And he was like, oh, I'm Tyler, and I'm also John's friend. They talked for a few minutes. Tyler was with some guy.

Did it look like a date? John asked. It didn't strike me as a date because the other guy was pretty ugly, Alexandra said. Short, glasses, swarthy. Plus, no vibe. Oh my God, I haven't seen John in forever, in like a month, Tyler said. Well, you should just IM him, he's on IM all day, she said. Then he said something about how he couldn't get into the party so Alexandra and her friend gave the two of them their wristbands.

John figured he got the text for cover. Like, Tyler's "early morning"? Not so early apparently. So Tyler was front-dooring the fact that Alexandra would probably tell John about Tyler being out.

But then, in talking it over with Fred, they decided that maybe Tyler was just completely oblivious.

"That asshole," Chad said when he heard about this.

So John hadn't responded to the last two texts. Then on Monday he got an email from Tyler. It went like: How about we get together this week? I still haven't seen "Julie and Julia." We work close together, I'm at 24th and 6th. See you soon, Tyler.

So John wrote back, like a day later: Sure. How about Thursday.

Tyler wrote something back, like, Thursday sounds great, and supposedly there's something fun at Galapagos?

And John wrote back: Out there? You? I'll believe it when I see it! And he mentioned there was some HBO party that night too, and there'd be free drinks and stuff and they could start there.

And Tyler wrote back: Can you bring a date?

And John wrote back: Yes, but it looks a little crappy, but it could be fun.

Tyler wrote back: "Or you can ask Alexandra if there are any cool fashion shows. J'adore models."

John didn't respond. J'adore models! Really. Then an hour later, Tyler wrote: "Whatever we do will be fun! Can't wait to catch up."

John thought this last email was pretty nice.

THE THING ABOUT not thinking about a bad thing was that when you tried not to think about it, then all you could do was think about it, until, finally, the brain slipped, and then you succeeded, you actually didn't think about it anymore, except that didn't last forever. Then a moment would come when you'd sit up in bed in a horror in the dark, and you couldn't help but think about it. But then you'd try to comfort yourself back to sleep, and then you'd forget again.

EDWARD WAS SUPPOSED to live with Amy for October. But that had fallen through. So was this never going to happen? They hadn't seen each other in two weeks. What would he do for money? Edward was making like 250 dollars a week, maybe a little less. Was he going to save up for an apartment with that? He needs to move to the City, John thought. He kept going back and forth to his parents' house.

The thing about getting to know someone was that it took so long to understand what they were really like from the inside, from their side.

John and Chad were going to throw a birthday party, and Edward was going to just happen to be in town. Diego kept saying he was a "maybe" because of John. John hoped everyone would show up, and by "everyone," he

meant everyone to whom he had a lingering romantic at-
tachment. They'd all take Adderall, a popular drug that
helped you pay attention.

Jason had discovered Adderall in college. He was pre-
scribed it because he had so much trouble concentrat-
ing. Well, but who doesn't? is what Jason thought. He
didn't know what these things were that doctors gave
you pills for: Restless leg syndrome? Seasonal disorder?
You can't sleep? Of course people were depressed, they
lived in a terrible place where it isn't sunny. That was
the same thing with attention deficit disorder, Jason
thought, which is what the Adderall was to treat. The
kids are unfocused? Sure, they're kids. But all that said,
he didn't really object to these sorts of pharmacological
interventions. Jason's doctor was particularly committed
to pharmacology and tended to solve every problem with
a prescription. Jason didn't necessarily subscribe to that
philosophy but he also didn't want to go to a doctor who
didn't subscribe to that. He didn't want to be lectured
to by a nanny when he was in pain and needed some
OxyContin or whatever. Maybe you need two doctors,
Jason thought. A real doctor and then a friendly doctor.
Somewhere in the middle was the Adderall. The pills
were a stand-in; they were a crutch, a goad, a spark plug,
a fix, an idea.

"IS EVERYONE WATCHING the Yankees game?" Edward asked. This was at a party.

"Who cares. It's so stupid," Jason said.

"John has forced me to watch football two or three times," Edward said.

"He forced me to watch baseball once," Jason said. "I didn't know what was— I mean, baseball I can understand at least. Football, it's so incomprehensible. It just starts and stops?"

"I felt like I was retarded because he kept trying to explain it to me," Edward said. "All those things about 'downs'? I was okay watching them run around, but any time there was any kind of numerical—"

"No, the point system is nonsense!" Jason said.

"Oh, that's okay," Edward said.

"Well, like you throw it through the 'U' thing and that's like seven points? I think?" Jason said.

"No, I think it's like one," Edward said. "Or three?"

"Oh. I don't even care obviously. At this point I've gone so far over the top," Jason said.

"I think it's like six if you get a touchdown, then it's a chance if you go through the thingie and then you get an extra one," Edward said.

"That just seems so worthless," Jason said. "I think you should get a lot of points if you go through that 'U' thing, not just one. Who wants one fucking point? I don't. I want seven."

SO EDWARD FINALLY had come to town, and he and Amy hosted a small gathering, in the afternoon.

Outside, after, no one could figure out where to go.

"It's so hard to make friends now," Rebecca said. Rebecca worked as a tutor, just like Chad. She'd been working at a job but had gotten fired. Now she was in a bit of a holding pattern, just like Chad, just like a lot of people. The difference was she was handily rich, regarding which she was super conscious. She knew that, unlike a lot of people, she was insulated from disaster.

Amy looked at her. "You're twenty-six!" Amy said.

"You're twenty-seven!" Rebecca said.

"I'm twenty-eight now," Amy said.

Rebecca pulled out her phone. Then she just looked at it.

"I don't even know who to text," she said.

Edward had told John: I'm going to be in the City tonight, so can we please see each other? But John didn't get off work till very late, and he sent Edward a text: Hey, it's really late, I'm going to bed. And Edward sent a text: Lemme buy you one drink, I'm in your neighborhood, I can get there fast. So, fine, how fast? John asked. And

Edward said, gimme three minutes. It took him a good bit longer than that, but they had a drink, then went to the deli to buy cigarettes. So let's just go have a drink at my house, John said. Where were you tonight? John said, on the way. Well, I was at Jason's house, Edward said. Sneaky: He hadn't been in the neighborhood at all.

So was this active pursuit? It was definitely active interest. John thought they could reach a good place if they talked about taking it really slow. Not that "slow" didn't mean that every time they saw each other, they didn't end up in bed! But they could work their way through it. They both needed to figure out if they both wanted it. He didn't even have a home, John thought.

CHAD'S BIRTHDAY WOULD be at midnight. It was windy and dark. They were at a very loud bar. It had a smoking section with bars all around it—actual bars, like in a prison—and concrete walls, but an open shaft in the ceiling with the moon up there. It was chilly, and everyone was shell-shocked.

But there were two birthdays to celebrate. "And John's is next week?" Jason asked. Jason had gotten drunk last night and, oddly enough, gone back to Amy's to crash, and then he got up really late and almost didn't go to work.

"Shall we go say hello to the birthday boys?" Edward said. The birthday boys were glued to the bar.

The reason most everyone was shell-shocked was that John's new boss, Timothy, had quit, and the boss's best friend, Jacob, who was now the new number two, had quit too. This rather shattered the system of belief that the office had chosen to accept from Timothy. The lay-offs, the penny-pinching: Well, now what? The sacrifice for the good of the team? What people were feeling was betrayal, though they didn't know who to be mad at. Timothy had taken the job, been an executioner, and now he couldn't stomach it? That probably wasn't fair to Timothy though. For all anyone knew he'd been thrown out too. For all anyone knew, he'd saved them from worse. So then who would come in—someone from the outside, with no desire of protecting the staff? Lots of people from the company's office were there at the party, and they looked ashen. Amelia, in particular, looked like she'd been hit in the stomach. And it was all supposed to be a secret, except it wasn't really a secret, and why should it be a secret anyway?

"You know what Gilda Radner said, what her book was?" John said. "*It's Always Something.* I'm not telling anyone on staff," John said.

"It doesn't matter, everyone's going to fucking know

in like five minutes," one of his coworkers said. "It's so stupid."

"But I'm not going to tell anyone on staff," John said.

"Can I have a cigarette, somebody?" his coworker said.

"Hey!" John said. "What's up, Timmy?"

Timothy had stumbled by.

They were all out in this smoking area, there was a hard breeze through the bars all around, and rock music was blaring.

"Are you under the impression this is all over in like a week?" his coworker asked.

"No, the way it was described to me was the end of the year."

"Yeah right," his coworker said.

"Do you think it's bullshit on that one?" John asked.

"No, no, I mean, I think it's end of the year or whatever, but don't you feel like this trigger has been pulled before? I think it's real, but do you know what I mean?"

"Here's what I was saying a second ago," John said. "Here's what I said. Talking to Timothy, I said, bullshit, you've told me you quit like eighty times before."

"But then you talked to Jacob?"

"And then Jacob—"

"Jacob kicked me in the face today." That was a meta-phor.

"And I was like, fuck you," John said.

"I went in to see Jacob and I said, 'Do I need a new career?' And Jacob was like, 'Yeah, actually, you do.' What should I do with myself?"

The drama! An acquaintance came in.

"Hi, guy," John said. "Very good." He was surrounding himself with everyone.

Then Trixie came in. "I'm underdressed, but I came out anyway," she said.

Sally had been out of town all week, so, Trixie said, she was making other people come into her office to hang out with her and entertain her. "I make Kyle come in and take off his glasses for a little while," she said. "I'm always lecturing Kyle about his twenties, and how he shouldn't waste them." She meant that, at this time, being young was still for making mistakes.

Then Timothy and Jacob came again to the smoking area.

"Oh no. God. I came out here to get away from them. I can't do it. I mean I saw it coming this afternoon," said one of their coworkers. "Then I just went home. Because I was like, I need to run away from this right now. Because I knew I would see them here tonight. And I ate an entire fried chicken to fortify myself."

Timothy lurched back inside.

"Wow," someone muttered.

"Hi, I'm Trixie," Trixie said.

"I'm Edward."

"It's really nice to meet you."

"So you, you're John's boss, right?"

"I would not say 'boss,'" she said.

They talked about work things for a while.

"I want to work so bad," Edward said.

Then why don't you have a job? someone asked.

"Well, because I've never had one," Edward said. "I was actually so pissed, because there was a big *New Yorker* story this week about the company I wanted to get in at, and now everyone's going to want to work at it. Whatever. I still feel more eminently qualified than everyone else but now it's like a big thing. So. John emailed me and was like, did you read this article? And I was like, I can't even read it! You need to be on the lookout for a job for me."

Are you talking to them at all? someone asked.

"Well, I know them all really well. I've never told them directly that I want to work there. They tried to hire me as a freelancer a couple of months ago, but it wasn't going to be enough money and it was too much work. And it was kind of like, you know, just hire me in-house please. But I don't think anybody's really hiring in-house right now! You don't have to give me all the benefits! I mean I do care about the health insurance, I guess, but they can just give me health insurance and— I do want to be like, by the way, 'I'm really cheap! Super cheap. You don't even have to give me vacation days.' "

"Remember that amazing *New Yorker* story from the late nineties about the guy who just showed up at a job and like started working?" Trixie asked.

"Wasn't that like on *Seinfeld* when George gets fired, or he quits in a rage or something, and they're like, just go back to work and see if anyone notices?" Edward said. "Yeah. I need a job."

"Oh my God, this is so depressing," Trixie said.

"I think I need better clothes too," Edward said. "I get so jealous of people talking about 'the weekend.' Because, like, my level of anxiety just remains the same, Monday through Sunday, I'm stressed about life. I'm just sick of this—I just want to be a hack! I don't want to do anything anymore. I just want to sell out. For nothing."

"Oh, Timothy and Jacob left!" someone said.

"Oh, Edward, this is my husband, Finn. Edward's been in our apartment." John had house-sat for them once, and Edward had come over.

"Just briefly," Edward said. "There were no wild parties or anything, I promise."

There was a pause.

"Oh, with John! I was like, old apartment? New apartment? The people before us?" Finn said.

"Somebody asked a question, like, is there like a Jewish mafia situation taking place outside your window?" Edward asked.

"The guy? In the car?" Trixie said.

"The guy in the car does seem like a mafia situation," Finn said.

"I think he's just getting free Internet from our building and watching Hulu," Trixie said. "Which is forbidden by his religion. Because he just watches the computer in his car all night."

"Some young Hasid comes and parks outside our building and watches YouTube all night," Finn said.

"That's like a short story," Edward said.

"Oh no, it's insane, we're going to have to talk to him," Trixie said. "Because it's like, every single night."

"I walked by drunk the other night and I was going to do it," Finn said.

"It's definitely not porn," Trixie said. "It's like TV. TV on his computer. Every night, in his, like, Lexus."

"He's going to break our heart when his Rumspringa comes to an end," Finn said.

"He is too old for Rumspringa," Trixie said. "He has a beard!"

"That's the Amish," Edward said.

"There's more than one problem," Finn said.

"My old college roommate, sort of my ex-boyfriend, well, my— My college roommate is studying to be a rabbi," Edward said. "He's like a real Yiddish scholar. He speaks, like, he's probably the last person in America who's not Hasidic to speak Yiddish as fantastically as he does. So we went to see Cat Power in McCarren Park a couple years ago? This guy, like, he's eccentric, and he's only gotten more eccentric since college. Afterward I was like, let's go to dinner, and it was Saturday night. And he was like, you know, Edward, it would really mean a lot to me if you would like come with me to South Williamsburg so I can talk to Hasids. Because you know he's fascinated with the culture, and he doesn't get that much chance to speak Yiddish."

"And it's going to help if you go with him?" Trixie said.

"And he wouldn't let you have dinner first?" Finn said.

"That was our compromise, I got to have dinner first," Edward said. "But I was wearing like, I was wearing like—"

"Men's low-rise pants?" Trixie asked.

"I was wearing cutoff booty shorts, and like one of those deep-V-neck American Apparel shirts that came down to like my belly button."

"That seems like the least appropriate outfit for talking to Hasids," Finn said.

"I know, I was like, I am not doing this; please please please. So finally we did. And it was really weird. And I think the guys we talked to—they were actually really excited to talk to him too, I think! It's weird to meet this young guy who was really interested in talking about religion and stuff with them. And they were asking all these trick questions."

"And so what did you do?" Finn asked.

"I just stood there and looked pretty," Edward said. "I was just hoping to find a husband basically."

"I don't think really—" Trixie said.

"I always wanted to have a minivan of my own," Edward said. "But while we were talking to them, there were all these people walking by giving them dirty looks. I think they were suspicious, that the guys talking to us were going to have people to answer to the next day."

"There's no question those guys had repercussions, but at the same time, those guys give dirty looks to anything they see on the street," Finn said. "It can be another Hasid couple."

"How about that guy who pulled over and asked directions the other day and then pulled over to ask someone else directions?" Trixie said.

"We actually get that a lot," Finn said.

TWO DAYS AFTER Timothy quit, the owner of the company called a meeting in the conference room. The owner brought in two platters of sandwiches. Ham sandwiches and one or two vegetarian options—a very soggy mozzarella, with portobello mushroom and zucchini. And tuna, or some unidentifiable fish salad, which really smelled and tasted of cat food. And Terra Chips, which were fried, thin-sliced vegetables.

The owner did not eat any of this food. Neither did the president of the company, the owner's henchman.

But Jacob, who'd quit as the number two, and another coworker, they went to town. Jacob was up and down, getting sandwiches, chomping loudly on chips. He actually hadn't even officially quit yet but he was going to, and everyone there except, most likely, the owner knew it, since he'd told them all.

The purpose of the meeting was to assure the staff that this transition was going to be just great. Everything was going to be just fine.

One person who worked there said he wished the owner could explain what he was envisioning, because he didn't understand what the owner wanted from the company.

The owner gave a long, meandering answer and closed with: "Does that answer your question?"

"Partially!" the employee said. He followed up. The

president of the company was sitting next to this employee. The president turned his chair to face the employee, staring directly into his face throughout the duration of the question.

And the owner's face as well! One employee said it was like a Gchat emoticon. He was always flat and neutral. But every once in a while, his expression cracked for a second and became just like an angry emoticon. His mouth would form a little "O" and his eyebrows would go all downward and slanty.

Timothy was sitting right there in the meeting, but that didn't stop the owner from saying things like, "We'll finally have a good leader."

Finally someone asked, "What if you don't find someone in time?" Timothy would be leaving at the end of the year.

"I'm sure Timothy will stay on till whenever we are ready," the owner said. Jacob, the number two, turned and looked at Timothy, mock seriously, as if to say something he wasn't going to say.

One of the higher-ups on the staff suggested that things were so tight, that so many people were doing two or three jobs at the company, that they couldn't afford to lose anyone more. This meant that everyone now was irreplaceable.

"I had a professor at Harvard," the owner said, "who had a plaque on his desk." The plaque, he said, was engraved with a quote that said something to the effect of: The fields of battle are littered with the bodies of irreplaceable men.

There was silence in the room for a while. A few people tried not to laugh. One of them distracted herself by singing, in her head, a song by Beyoncé called "Irreplaceable."

Everyone—that is, everyone who still cared—wanted to know if there would be further layoffs. The owner said that he didn't know because he didn't interfere in the operations of the company. This wasn't true at all because of course he did, not least by setting the budgets that allowed for various numbers of employees being paid various amounts of money.

The owner held forth on business ethics for a while. Also, there was a bright spot in dealing with the staff, the owner said, for some unknowable reason. He compared his business favorably with another company, a union shop. That was a workplace in which the nonmanager employees formed their own organization so as to bargain, together, for the best possible terms of employment. That other business, a well-known one in the same industry, was hobbled, he said, "with their stupid union."

One of the employees was so upset by this that she started crying.

John spent the entire meeting pretending to check emails on his mobile phone. The staff sitting behind him could see that he was actually just playing a low-quality game called BrickBreaker whose ancestry could be traced to the earliest computers, in which the goal was to control a virtual ball that breaks through variously configured walls of virtual bricks.

Jacob and Timothy left and spent the rest of the day getting drunk, talking about what they'd do next. The rest of the staff went immediately outside and smoked. "It'll be okay," said one young employee.

"Nope," John said. "It's not okay." He was really upset. Sally told him about her friends' new kittens to cheer him up. Edward was, of course, planning to spend the night that night, but John said he just wanted to be alone and that he'd send Edward off to Jason's couch, or whoever's couch Edward was supposedly sleeping, or usually, really, not sleeping, on.

Edward, in the end, did come over but then he went out again. John stayed in and stared at the TV.

WHEN PEOPLE MADE a thing for the first time, they could claim the thing, and the method of making it, as belonging solely to them.

For instance, someone made a nine-inch-long metal

stick, with little serrations all facing one way, and with a handle. And people were to use that to carve off tiny flaky bits of cheese. It had patent number 5100506, and the patent covered several surprising techniques, techniques that you might not expect for something as simple as grating cheese. In the technique, a whole metal file was formed, with "a plurality of cutting teeth chemically etched in the metal blank" and "the etching treatment which is used to form the cutting teeth being applied in one direction only from the back surface toward the front surface of the metal blank."

So this tiny thing, it was a significant, possibly profitable but never discussed little invention, owned by three people jointly and assigned to a company based far outside the City. The world was absolutely crammed full of these sorts of things. Handy things, little things—each with little numbers on them, leading back to the patent, the marker of the ownership of an idea or a process or a way. Some people worked nearly every day to make things that would gain a patent. Some people would go their whole lives without patenting something, without the idea of doing so even occurring to them. But those to whom it did often produced the patented idea under the care of their employers. They were hired to make things, and so in the course of this paid employment, the inventions were retained by the company. It was like most all work. All the ideas, thoughts, contributions, labor, materials— that was what the employer bought from the worker.

But really also still, for him- or herself, anybody could make a thing, or a sketch of a thing, and then file for a patent, which would be granted, if it was an original thing that he or she had made.

CHAD AND DIEGO'S new apartment was great. They were really getting to know each other from the perspective of the other person. Diego was great, Chad thought.

Except. "Diego does this thing when he cracks eggs, he leaves the empty shells in the egg carton," Chad said. "I was like, why do you do this? He was like, 'You're trying to, like, control me.' I mean my tone might have been a little more aggressive? It might have been less of a question and more of, like, you are so fucking weird for doing this. Why! Why! They smell and it's just weird. I feel like in the refrigerators of the insane are egg cartons full of empty shells. Like people who collect sugar packets from restaurants. Like my great-grandmother, who died, and in a closet were hundreds of thousands of sugar packets. He's not a particularly annoying person! Anyway I see him less now than when we didn't live together. It's fine. It's good. I'll come home and he's already asleep and he'll leave before I'm awake."

EVERYONE WHO OWNED sweaters took them down from the back of closets or out of trunks or from under whatever clothes had piled up on top of them. The first few trees dashed off their leaves and were suddenly lone and bare. It happened fast. The harbor turned cold; the warmer water retreated down the coast. A fog would coat the bridges and buildings, and long, low warnings would boom out over the bays. It was in the fog that the City became small. It was easy to forget the sea, and how close it was, until the fog horns traveled all across the City, their sound and a chill both shuddering up over the hills from the water.

JOHN SHUT OFF the part of himself that cared about his job. He felt so much better now that he'd made a conscious decision to not care about his job at all. Who would want to care?

He also felt better because Edward just kept not leaving.

Really it was because he was angry about the way people were being treated at work that he felt he couldn't care. People confused these states sometimes. When he was angry, or wanted to avoid something, he, like many people, always expressed it by saying, "I don't care." But they did care.

This was a reasonable but dangerous attitude about work in trying times. If you didn't do very well at your job, you could lose your job. And if you lost your job, you could maybe not find a new one. Around the country, the "Help Wanted" listings often said things like "no unemployed applicants" or "no long-term unemployed." That is because humans were made so that they often only wanted things that other people wanted. And even apart from that: You just had more value if people wanted you. This was often true in love as well.

And if you didn't have any value, you could just disappear, like being dropped through a hole in the floor. Edward, for instance, with no real source of money, at least had his parents' house in another city to go live in. Where could John go?

So he did a decent enough job at work. But it was too upsetting, the workplace too gross and now all twisted. Everyone spent all day in the office leaping over these chasms that'd opened up. Most people there were looking for a job, but there weren't really any to be had.

John thought Edward was great though. Edward for some reason was always convinced, from the very first day, even when they weren't really "together," that John would cheat on him. John thought Edward wouldn't cheat on him. This belief was solely predicated on John's belief that such a thing would never happen to him. But he realized that wasn't trust. What John thought about was how guilty he would feel if he were the one cheating. He'd have to call Edward right away and confess. One night he was out, and Dieter from work was there, and John was like, wow, there are so many hot guys here, it's all so tempting. And Dieter turned to him, all serious: "John, you've got a really good thing going. Don't mess that up." And that seemed simple but it made a lot of sense.

John thought about his recent months in terms of a popular movie called *Jurassic Park*, in which some people had gotten stuck on an island where scientists had cloned extinct dinosaurs and set them loose in a new ecosystem. When a writer made up futures, it was called "science fiction," at the time. To lure in one of the scary dinosaurs in the movie, the trapped people had hung up this goat, to lure the dinosaur in with the scent. But the dinosaur wasn't interested. And the lead character in *Jurassic Park* realized: The T. rex doesn't want to be fed. Instead he wants to hunt. John thought that he was like this dinosaur.

ONE NIGHT, JOHN and Edward just stayed at home, alone together, and smoked a lot of pot, and somehow, John ended up all tangled in Christmas lights, all shiny and colored and spectacular and hilarious, Edward lying back on the broken-slatted twin bed, just laughing.

JOHN AND JASON rehashed their Halloween night. Halloween was an ancient pagan holiday in honor of the dead now observed by dressing as sexy animals or in sexy workplace uniforms. They had gone to a magazine party—that is to say, a party thrown by a magazine—and then ended up at Sugarland, the long and dark and cavernous bar.

"Remember that guy Reed who was flirting with Edward very openly? Ugh, I hated that guy so much," John said.

"Oh, he had like an Afro?" Jason said.

"Yes, and he was like, hi, my name's Reed," John said.

"Oh, I didn't like that person," Jason said.

"Ugh, I hated him. I was looking at him like I was going to kill him," John said.

"Do you know that person?"

"No! I was like, don't talk to Edward!"

"People are allowed to talk to Edward," Jason said.

"I got very upset. Then Edward was like, oh you know, there's also a Brazilian guy in the bathroom or whatever. And I'm like, a Brazilian man in the bathroom?"

"They didn't like me as much that time," Jason said.

"They did like you! Remember that guy who was staring at you? The Boy Scout?"

"I'm just not that kind of pervo."

"But you have to be in a situation like that."

"Well, I was a pervo later," Jason said.

"I had never seen anything like it," John said. "It was like ass in the air, everywhere you looked. It was packed. The cruisiest place I've ever been."

"I was so un-hot!" Jason said.

"You were not un-hot."

"No, not me but everyone else."

"Oh my God, there were a lot of hot guys there!"

"Were there?"

"Oh, that was the other guy! Dave's roommate was all over him," John said.

"Dave is the biggest whore in the world," Jason said.

"No, his roommate!"

"No, I know!"

"Oh, that one's a whore?"

"They're both whores!"

"You know how I know?" John said. "Because he Facebook friended me and I looked at the pictures of him."

"Oh, I know, he has those hungry eyes!"

"He looks like Milhouse from *The Simpsons*," John said.

"He has Milhouse-without-glasses eyes. Like these beady little eyes."

"Edward looked great that night. He wasn't wearing any costume. I got too dressed up," Jason said.

"So did I," John said. "I was a bandit. Did I look okay?"

"Yeah, no, you totally," Jason said. "I was Sonia Sotomayor. Or Rachel Maddow. I kept changing it."

"And any time I smoked, or any time Edward smoked, I said, 'This is Smokey and the Bandit,'" John said.

The magazine party they went to first had allegedly cost 150,000 dollars.

"But the open bar was, like, a pitcher of margaritas," Jason said.

"And Colt 45," John said. "That party, it sucked. Sugarland was fun though. I was really drunk, I had to go home. Edward was so proud of himself. He was like, you know those nights when you have your mojo? I feel like I had my mojo. And I was like, yeah, I know. He looked great. What was Edward saying he was at the end of the night? Oh, he was like, 'I'm Precious.'"

"Yeah, no," Jason said. "I dunno, it felt kind of depressing toward the end."

"Nobody knew what the time was. I didn't know if it was two a.m. or four a.m., the time kept changing. Plus I was so drunk. I only had like four beers and I was so wasted. I had sushi! I was on so much medication because I was sick."

"Adderall?" Jason asked.

"I had a Tic Tac or two," John said. "But like. Speaking of! Do you have it?"

"Oh yeah," Jason said.

"Oh, I'm not doing it tonight! I'm not doing it tomorrow," John said. "But soon. Soonsies!"

NOW THE OWNER of John's company got married to a princess, of sorts, though technically she was becoming her own king. Family and friends and business associates came from far but particularly from near to observe the nuptials. John's owner's intended bride wore white, a rather recent tradition indicating purity, particularly— and this will sound vulgar!—intactness of virginity. That was something that wasn't talked about; it was considered nobody's business, except for the bizarre wearing of white. The former mayor of the City came. The Mayor did not. Various owners of enormous businesses attended—a very, very rich foreign man who owned newspapers and television stations around the world, and others like him. The groom gave the bride a ring of shiny rocks of a high price.

They were married on property, a sporting grounds

associated with her father, who had reinvented kingship in his own way. Once he had made buildings, but with the growing cachet of his buildings, he found a way to not have to make the buildings himself any longer, but simply to sell his name to other building makers so that these buildings carried his imprimatur and he got paid for the use of it. There was an incredible lesson about commerce in there. His name was a trademark, which was like a patent. So the bride's father had perhaps the most inventively diffuse kingdom of them all: People paid him to allow them to build vertical kingdoms with his name on them, and then other people paid those builders to reside in them.

It seemed very strange when you started to think about it all.

In any event these two were in love, and so they pledged to spend their lives together until they died. Or until they didn't want to be married anymore—that was currently considered legitimate as well. The whole "until you die" thing might have just been an old leftover thing that people said because they were supposed to.

THE OWNER OF Kevin's company, who was not at the wedding of his estranged cousin, threw a party on the night before the election.

The party was in a weird storefront that had been built out in the most elaborate way. There were like these portals, and angular walls, and weird little passageways onto the street. It was very futuristic and had many dark corners.

"John, you're going to get banned," Edward said. John was smoking out one of the portals, but he had a beer so he couldn't step outside onto the street either, because it was against the law to drink on the street.

"I'm not going to get banned," he said.

Kevin had grown an enormous brushy mustache. "I was saying, does this tear off? And he got so upset! He was like, no, I just grew it," John said. "I was like, it looks good, and he was like, okay."

"I'm going to take a vacation. I'm going to take like three days off next week. Whatever," John said.

Jacob at work—because they were still riding out their time in the office until at least the end of the year—had told a staffer that his own other part-time job was basically finding a new job, and so everyone in the office was of equal dispiritedness. They were taking the vacation days they could. And Timothy and Jacob had invited everyone over for dinner. Trixie had told them she was out of town. Sally told them she had plans. No one was going to come to dinner.

"It sounds like the Kübler-Ross stages," Edward said.

"Are you going to grab another beer? If you could grab me one," John said. Okay, Edward said. "Oh, you're a good guy," John said. "Tomorrow, Election Day!" John said to Jason. "I'm not voting. I have no time to do it tomorrow."

"I don't think I could get into law school," Edward said. Apparently he was just considering his options.

"Why does this party have to end at nine?" John said. "You have to eat."

"I do?" Edward said.

"You're wasting away," Jason said.

"Why weren't you online most of the day?" John said.

"I was in the downtown office. It was a madhouse. It was totally crazy today," Jason said.

"Did John tell you about our dinner?" Edward said. He and John had gone out with Amy and Amy's boyfriend. "Amy's mom, who's like the least fun person in the world, after she met him, she said to Amy, I really like your boyfriend, but let me ask you a question: Has he ever had fun in his life?" John didn't really get along with Amy. She didn't like to spend a lot of time with Edward and John together either. The real reason, which Edward and John didn't really know or pretended not to know, was that she was horrified about how they were constantly groping and kissing each other. Also she thought John was too young for Edward and also too much of a player. "I didn't even notice what a bitch she was being. It bounces off me," Edward said. Also at the dinner, Amy was going on about how John's boss, Timothy, was totally in the owner's pocket. "And John was like, I don't think so, and she was like, uh-huh. Also she was like, 'Oh, you, you're so naive,'" Edward said. So that had all of John's hackles up. "I made really good cookies," Edward said.

"I think I pissed Chad off yesterday," he said. "They were having their nightly phone wrap-up and I piped up from the background. I was revealing my presence and he was like, 'I've gotta go!' But I love Chad. He's so cute. By 'cute' I mean very attractive. He's a very loud talker. Former drama club member perhaps."

Edward was mad that he'd never taken advantage of his last relationship, apart from having had a nice apartment in the City and all that. Aric traveled constantly, for one thing. "He's gone at least a week out of every month. He goes like amazing places. I was always like too poor to go. And he was always sort of discouraging about me coming. But I do regret it. He didn't trust me to fend for myself. It's probably fair. I told John the other day: Before we broke up, this girl was begging him for his sperm. And now I have this terror. Doesn't that seem like a reasonable thing to do? In the wake of a breakup, to have a baby? And that'd be the worst thing."

Well, maybe not the worst thing.

"One time I left the Cock," John said, "and there was this cabdriver, and he was like, do you like that place? And I was like, no. And he was like, do guys go there? And I'm like . . . yeah. He was like, a lot of guys like to go there, right? Keep in mind he's driving and turning around to look at me all the time. So I rolled down all the windows so it was like a noisy wind. And I kept being like, 'I can't hear what you're saying!'"

"How come cabdrivers never hit on me?" Edward said.

"Oh my God," Jason said, "it's like the second time."

"Am I just fucking repulsive?" Edward said.

"No comment," Jason said.

"It's like the same as how I always get so mad about never seeing anyone have sex in the steam room," Edward said. "I feel like it's like I walk in and everyone's like, oh God, he's here. Halt!"

"Never mind," John said.

"I always see it happen," Jason said.

"Everyone's always complaining about it!" Edward said. "I mean I haven't actually been to the gym in years, but back when I did, it was the Sports Club on Fourteenth Street."

"You belonged to the Sports Club at some point?" John asked.

"I know it's hard to imagine," Edward said.

"I remember," Jason said.

"I can't imagine it, when did this happen?" John asked.

"It was back in my—" Edward said.

"Oh, your virile days?" John said.

"No, not my virile days, my days of milk and honey," Edward said. "When I was super rich. When I was just throwing money around everywhere."

"I've heard about these days," John said.

"They were really fun," Edward said.

"We were both so rich," Jason said.

"I bought so many videogames," Edward said.

"I bought so many suits," Jason said.

"Oh, I didn't go that far," Edward said.

"Everyone's poor," John said. "Maybe I'll be able to change that soon, hey."

"Jason came up with the best Halloween costume after the fact," Edward said.

"What what what," John said.

"Brooke Astor," Edward said.

"Oh, that'd be brilliant but you need a dachshund or three," John said.

"I was thinking more of a pee-stained nightgown," Jason said. "Because everyone wants to see Mrs. Astor. Even in a nightgown covered in urine. Did she have dachsies?"

"Oh my God, I think she left like millions of dollars to her dachshunds," John said.

"Didn't Leona leave all that money to—"

"Oh, Leona did that too," John said.

These were the names of rich people who they didn't personally know.

"Wait, didn't someone tell me that story about Leona," Edward said, "that she would do laps in the pool every day. In her, you know, personal indoor pool. And she would have a servant standing at each end and when she came up for air at the end of the lane, they'd drop a shrimp in her mouth."

"That cannot be true," Jason said.

"This sounds like an embellishment by the person telling the story, but I think she would also say, 'Feed the fishie.'"

"That sounds wonderful," John said.

"It sounds a little less than believable to me," Jason said.

"Isn't there a bit of a problem with eating and swimming?" John said.

"Maybe it was only at one end of the pool," Edward said.

"Maybe they were baby shrimp," Jason said.

"I guess you would get full pretty quickly," Edward said.

"Kevin! Say hello!" John said.

"I'm working!" Kevin said.

"Take a load off!" Jason said.

"I'm the point person at this thing! I have a clipboard!" Kevin said. "I'm administering!"

Jason started hacking. "I'm going to the doctor on Election Day!" he said. "I stopped smoking. It's really bad. I'm going to my allergy-asthma doctor tomorrow."

"Why do these cigarettes taste so bad?" Edward said.

"Here, let me see," Jason said.

"It's really like metallic. I came up with the best idea," Edward said. "When I go back home, I'm going to drive in my parents' car and get cartons and cartons of cigarettes."

"And then sell them?" Jason asked.

"And then sell them," Edward said. "They cost like two dollars there."

"You're going to be so rich," Jason said.

"It's the kind of thing I'm probably too lazy to do," Edward said.

Chad wandered in. Everyone screamed. He went to get a beer.

Then a crazy man wandered in too and started ranting about the Mayor, and how awful the Mayor was, and how the Mayor secretly had a boyfriend.

"I haven't heard this!" John said.

"Is this a surprise?" the crazy man said. "In terms of his character, I mean, is this a surprise?"

"Well, he is such a bitch," Jason said.

Jason martyred himself for the group and let the crazy man isolate him from the rest. The guy said a lot of stuff about how the Jews were messing everything up, and how the Mayor was in league with Israel, which Jason didn't really enjoy. So then Edward very kindly took a turn.

Edward couldn't vote—he wasn't registered there. Chad was registered at his old address, and it would take him hours to get there, so he probably wouldn't go vote. John definitely wasn't going to vote tomorrow. Though maybe he was going to do a write-in. "I got really mad at him today," Jason said about John. "He nearly COL'd! Cried out loud! I am mad. Chad, are you going to—?"

"I actually might not vote," Chad said. "I've done a great deal to work for—"

"I've done a great deal as well!" John said.

"What!" Jason screamed. "What!" and started hacking.

"I've had a really long couple of weeks," John said.

Edward came back from the crazy man. "He told me if he was going to die tomorrow, if I was going to die tomorrow, my last, like my dying thing, my last—I have completely lost—" Edward said.

"Maybe you need more Adderall," Jason said.

"I have completely lost my capacity for language," Edward said. "Basically he told me he would take a vial of sulfuric acid and throw it in the Mayor's face."

"If you only have one day, there's only so much you can do. You have to find the Mayor, you have to find the sulfuric acid . . ." Jason said.

"He wouldn't want to kill him. He just wanted the Mayor to look in the mirror and see the ugliness inside every day," Edward said.

They discussed this for a while.

"And he's so hideous as it is!" someone said. "Why hasn't he had more plastic surgery to make himself more attractive? Or at least a D enlargement."

"I bet he has a big dick."

"No way."

"Well, he's so small that at least—"

"Yeah, I bet it looks bigger than it is. Because he is a big dick."

"I actually kind of enjoy talking to those crazy people," Edward said. "I got a lot of practice with those conversations when I used to sneak into bars in high school and would always attract the one oldest, craziest person in the room. I would always leave happy!"

"Because you were a little less crazy?" John said.

"No, it was something to do. It was better than standing in a corner by yourself."

"I'd rather writhe in the corner quite frankly," John said. "Writhing in the corner!"

"Nobody puts Eddie in the corner," Jason said.

"Many people have put Eddie in the corner over the years," Edward said.

Edward was staying in town for the next forty-eight hours. But that expiration date meant John was sad. "I told him he should just live in my apartment. He got all happy," John said. "He wants to. I got mad at him today because he didn't stay in my apartment today. He went to Jason's. He had to get his laptop. I was like, just stay with me! My cousin doesn't care. My cousin loves Edward. For two weeks! Then he can get his own apartment. I like the kid around. He'll just stay for two weeks. Well, he has to get money. I'll give him money! I'll save, I won't smoke or something. We smoke so much more. He's so cute. My God. He looks— I'm so happy. He looks so good right now. He's such a loving little guy. It's good right now. I like the guy a lot."

THE NEXT DAY, Election Day, Jason was still so insanely ill. He was downtown at seven a.m., and the first thing he saw was this man having a total seizure on the street, convulsing, there was like blood on the street, he fell, ambulances came. Jason was really superstitious and this seemed to him like a bad omen. And then it turned out he had pneumonia. He kept pretending it was allergies and he didn't slow down for a second. Maybe it can't be good to go out every night, he thought.

And over the course of the day, the Mayor had gotten 585,466 votes.

His challenger had gotten 534,869 votes.

A total of 1,154,802 people's votes were counted.

There were 4,095,561 active registered voters in the City.

So only about 28 out of every 100 people who could vote did.

The challenger had won a significant majority of voters in distinct regions of the City. If those regions were like little cities, the Mayor wouldn't be the mayor there anymore.

The Mayor's team had played it like it was an easy sail to victory. But it wasn't any such thing. He could have lost quite easily. That was why he'd spent all that money.

So they'd all been hoodwinked! Or, more accurately, they'd let themselves be hoodwinked.

JOHN'S COMPANY DECIDED to throw a party to announce the hiring of the new boss of the office.

The party was held at the swank downtown store of a foreign purse and leather goods maker. It was on the second floor, where they kept the good stuff. The staff came, all draggy, without much interest. There is only so much anxiety or resentment that can be maintained for so long. Sooner or later, one develops a tolerance.

Timothy was there. He was all political smiles. Their old boss Thomas was there too. He'd been talked into introducing the new boss. Lots of people there hadn't seen him for a while. It was rather like running into your father by surprise in a busy airport. He was a mad kind of gleeful, all glittering, almost frightening.

The new boss swam around the room. He almost looked the part: a grown-up in a suit. Tall and wooden, he wore a red string around his wrist, and his pants didn't cover his bare ankles. It was impossible not to think that he hadn't even started yet and was in over his head.

There was a coin purse for sale in the leather goods store. It cost 195 dollars. It measured about four inches by three inches by one inch. Apart from that being two or three days' worth of salary for some of the employees present, also you would need 9.75 pounds of quarter-dollar coins to fill the coin purse with enough money to pay for it.

JOHN'S DESK OVERSPILLED with envelopes.

A billing statement for Direct Loans. For this bill, the total balance due was 40,337.26 dollars.

This bill was due on the seventh of each month. His monthly payment for this loan was 152.22 dollars.

This particular bill said that it was sixty days overdue. "We are preparing to report this loan(s) to national credit bureaus," it said.

There was also another letter from Direct Loans, for a bill six months after the last one. In this bill, it said that his total balance was now 41,319.91 dollars.

That meant that, despite a few payments, and because of interest and late fees, his total outstanding loan from Direct Loans was now 982.65 dollars more than it had been six months previous.

There was a letter from "Diversified Collection Services Inc. a Performant Company." It was sent on behalf of the creditor called United Guaranty Commercial Insurance Company of North Carolina. The balance due, they wrote to say, was 13,827.27 dollars. They would take from John's bank account, they wrote, two weeks later, the amount of 165 dollars.

And if he paid them that amount each month for the next eighty-three months, he would then, seven years later, provided there was no interest or penalties added, owe them only 132.27 dollars.

It had become impossible to tell from the statements which bill was for which loan or debt. The Diversified Collection Services might be servicing a credit card bill, or a student loan.

For instance, there was a statement from FIA Card Services. FIA was formerly named MBNA but had changed its name four years ago, after being bought by Bank of America the year previous. At this time, Bank of America held more than 1 in 10 of each dollar that people in the country put in banks.

The letter from FIA Card Services may or may not have been about the same debt referenced by Diversified Collection Services Inc. Their note arrived the next month, noting a debt with a balance of 11,930.56 dollars but with a "new balance" of 12,220.23 dollars, as it was "past due."

Still, much of this debt was student loans, parceled out to different lenders and now, apparently, one or more collection agencies as well.

There were his FFELP loans. Those were loans that were serviced through private companies, but that took subsidies from the government—and also the government insured much of these loans in case of default. It was a largely risk-free business, given that.

His Stafford FFELP loans, granted five years ago, were for 8,500 dollars of subsidized loans and 10,000 dollars of unsubsidized loans. The difference between the two was actually quite minor; it was that the "subsidized" loans were for people who fell below a certain income level, and so that, while they were in school, or when their loan payments later were temporarily deferred or defaulted upon, the government would pay for the interest that accrued.

His Perkins loan request, for professional school, was for 6,000 dollars. This was also due to a federal program, and only "needy" applicants could receive money for graduate school.

Also he had a private loan, a CitiAssist loan, for 15,000 dollars, from August of five years ago.

The government had been planning on changing how student loans were made. What happened with student loans was that the government actually subsidized the companies that loaned money to people to go to school, but the lenders got to keep the profits from the loans.

Instead now people thought: Why not give the money directly to colleges and to students, for tuition?

The loan companies hired more firms to go down to the Capital and engage in lobbying, the practice of persuading policy makers.

One firm put out twenty-two billion dollars in loans just in the year previous, and also spent eight million dollars on these lobbying efforts—twice what they'd spent the year before. Ten million students received loans in the year overall.

The government would, if they eliminated or restructured companies like that one, retain eighty billion dollars over the next ten years.

Well, maybe it would happen, maybe it wouldn't.

All told, at the end of this year, John's debt added up to about 15,000 dollars for college, 40,000 for professional school and about 14,000 in credit card debt during school, almost 70,000 dollars all in, a small percentage of which was paid down. Who could even begin to start worrying about a thing like this? That was what desk drawers were for.

DAYS LATER, JASON still had what he described as "total pneumonia." He went to the doctor and the doctor said, "Can you breathe really deep please?" And Jason said, "Well, no?" But he was on the mend, mostly. He was trying to drink through it. John was in a terrible mood and was pounding beers. It had just gotten dark, and everyone wanted to huddle inside. They were at a friend's house, and Sally had come along after work.

"I apologized both Tuesday night and Wednesday morning. I will never not vote again," John said.

"I apologize as well," Sally said. "Here's the situation. I

moved three years ago, and I still have not changed where I'm registered. That was the first time I'd ever not voted. But I actually really wish I had."

"Samesies," John said.

It really had been so close.

"I said this to Chad: If everyone knew how close it was going to be, and everyone had to revote, everyone would come out—and he'd still win," John said.

"It was so crazy at my polling place," Jason said. "The Democratic Party guy in Brooklyn? The city council-woman was his protégé. She's like the first Dominican woman elected to everything. They had some disagree-ment about some zoning thing. And she was on the side of the community and he was on the side of the develop-ers. And she's dead to him now. So he like hates her, he totally opposes her. And she won the primary against his handpicked administrative assistant. So she won in the primary, and he, as the head of what is perhaps the larg-est Democratic Party organization in the country, is not supporting the candidate! He's supporting this ridiculous woman. She literally was like his assistant. So he really got all the troops out. There were these warring factions outside my polling place. There were like no voters! But maybe hundreds of people! It was crazy.

"I almost miss the Bush years in some ways,

personally," Jason said. "Well, I married well then. Every time I watch *Mad Men*, I'm like, I totally saw this episode but it was way better when it was on *The Sopranos*. I was like, this really reminds me of something I really like, but way better, with Edie Falco. Or *The Simpsons*! Edward was explaining to me—I mean I watch it and I like it but I don't know all the backstory—and he was explaining to me Don Draper's identity, and I was like, this is the exact same story as Principal Skinner. Right? In the war? I was shocked."

"Oh my God," Sally said.

"You know what was on like HBO3 or something? *Apollo 13*," John said.

"Oh my God, I totally met that astronaut once," Jason said. "Jim?"

"What was that like?" John asked.

"Oh, it was in high school. So I was like, I don't care."

"Right? 'Oh, so you went to space,'" Sally said.

"Yeah, like: 'Fuck you,'" Jason said. "He seemed very nice, I don't know. He was some old white man."

"Jason and I both have an unhealthy obsession with the Oscars?" John said. "What we do is play a game with each other. We have two different versions. For me, Jason will name a year, and I'll have to pantomime a scene from the movie that won Best Picture. Jason will be like, 1962, then you have to do a scene. I'm horrible after *Gladiator*, I don't know what happened, but tell me 1974 and I'm ready to go."

"Oh, I know, *Godfather II*," Jason said.

"Exactly. I like to do the scene on the ship, where he's looking at the Statue of Liberty, little Vito. And Jason is an expert on Best Actress and Best Supporting Actress—"

"1983," Sally said.

"Which one?"

"Best Actress."

"Shirley MacLaine," Jason said.

"That's *Terms of Endearment*?"

"That's kind of easy. Everyone knows that," John said.

"Was Debra Winger Supporting?"

"No, she was also Best Actress but lost," Jason said.

"Who were the other nominees?" Sally said.

"I don't know if I'm going to know this!"

"*Silkwood*?" John said.

"*Silkwood* was '83! Dolly!"

"Dolly!" John said. "Dolly was nominated."

John was trying to round people up to go out, as usual. Chad was out with Diego and resisting. John was saying mean things.

"He's not that big, right?" Sally asked. She'd never really met him. "Would you describe Chad's boyfriend as a large man?"

"No! I wouldn't say he's like a svelte person. I don't know!" Jason said.

"He's not a beast, but like," John said, "there was a picture, from my birthday party, that I put on Facebook, from the album in which you never existed?"

"But I was like there," Jason said.

"You were at the party. Look, I was hardly in any pictures! Kevin was in every picture. But like there's one of Diego that I couldn't include. The resolution couldn't fit. It was like, you've exceeded your amount. He was, like, this big, and then there was me on the side of him. I mean it was disgusting," John said.

"I mean he can't be that fat!" Jason said.

Chad texted. "What is Two Boots?" John said. "Oh, it's a pizza place? So Diego's eating pizza right now."

"Oh, of course," Jason said. "How many pies? No, I don't hate Diego as much as some people do."

"I don't know what you're talking about," John said.

"I didn't say you," Jason said.

"He's not as fat as Chris Christie," John said.

"I just feel like I'm not one to talk," Jason said.

John got tired of texting and so finally he called Chad, but Chad wasn't interested.

"Okay. Alright, well, we'll see each other sometime soon I guess," John said. "No, that's okay. Whenever!

Whenever, whenever. Whatever! I don't know what else to say, I'm not mad, whatever! Alright, I'll talk to you soon."

He hung up.

"Oh, he's pissed off with me. He was like, 'Oh, I'd really prefer the passive-aggressiveness be put to the side, okay?' He was like, 'Oh, Diego really wants to go home.'"

FINALLY, FINALLY, ONE morning Edward and John went to a health clinic to get their medical tests. They'd really put this off. John had tried as hard as possible not to think about this for as long as possible.

Health clinics existed because some people had health insurance and others did not, and so, as opposed to doctor's offices, clinics had a different, usually lower, rate of payment. Even though John had some health insurance, it was better for him to go there, and Edward didn't have any anyway. So they told them how much money they made, and the clinic told them what amount on their "scale" of prices they should pay for services.

Edward was anxious; John was cavalier. Edward, really, was anxious about this only because he'd been with John.

John got his negative test results forty-five minutes before Edward.

It was a long and excruciating forty-five minutes though.

But then Edward's results came back negative too. And they were very happy about this, but they could also feel the rush of relief. You could consider yourself lucky, or you could have some other made-up system of belief to make sense of things, but it didn't matter. Disasters happened.

And sometimes they didn't.

Monogamy is so nice, John said. It's so relaxing.

They went out to a party thrown by one of Jordan's exes. "You're a romantic," someone said to John, with surprise. They were standing outside on an old, old street. The paving stones were big gray stone blocks.

"I always was," he said. "You could have asked Edward that and he'd have said so."

"Blood brothers!" John said. John and Edward pressed their fingers against each other, but Edward couldn't remember which finger he'd given blood for his test from, so he just picked one.

THEN IT WAS that time already, winter was coming on, now all the trees were all dead again!

THERE WERE MORE than a hundred hearings every business day at the Transit Adjudication Bureau—more than twenty-five thousand in the year. About eight hundred of those hearings were for taking up too much space on the subway. This was sometimes the charge against the people who didn't have homes who tried to sleep on the trains.

For the first hearing, you would just show up. It seemed like nearly all the adjudicators were old women. So you would wait, and go to window after window, and wait some more, and then you would see someone, and everything would be recorded on old analog tapes.

Chad was stoked for his hearing. He was going to show the City that he couldn't be controlled. His ticketing officer actually did show up; everyone had told Chad that they never did. Chad got to question the officer. How could the police officer remember anything at this point? Chad remembered everything, in vivid detail, and Officer Vargas was in for a grilling. He recognized Chad's face but nothing else. Chad was sort of offended. Chad asked a few leading questions. "What was my foot doing?" The judge was very helpful—and in the end dismissed the case.

He was so excited. "Yes!" Chad said and hit the counter at the window. "Please do not hit the window," the clerk said. The judge, in her write-up, called Chad "consistant [sic], forthright and sincere." Chad had been cited before, for drinking on the platform, and had once been with someone who'd been cited for smoking on an open-air platform, so he could have looked like a repeat offender.

Everyone was getting sick as winter came on. Chad was so ill and dizzy during his hearing. Later he went to a friend's reading and had to run outside and throw up in a trash can. Everyone was coughing and hacking and throwing up all the time. It was a bright spot that the City paid to have trash receptacles available for public use on the street.

JOHN WAS AT work, so he was on Facebook, doing nothing, sending all the pictures on this one guy's account to Chad so they could laugh about them. This was the account of a professional guy, but in all his pictures he was pretty much shirtless and buff and showing off. And then John accidentally sent one to Max, a guy in the office. The problem with chat was that you would choose who you talked to from a list of everyone you had ever talked to, and it was easy to misfire, to click the wrong person from the list. It was equally easy to have a number of chat windows open and to type into the wrong little digital box. And Max was like, uh, what's this? And John was like, well, obviously that is from this guy's Facebook page! And Max was like, oh, I see, haha, that's the best! Anyway, John was looking at these pictures of this guy with all these other guys and realized, oh, I know this one here, I went on a date with him. He remembered some details about the guy, but that was it. No idea what his name was or what they had done. There was nothing left there to recall.

THE STAFF WAS back in Duke's for a going-away party, at last, in honor of Timothy and Jacob. They were finally leaving the company! The new boss was there, and Thomas, their old boss, had come back, but the owner hadn't been invited. And their old boss got up and made a speech.

"You guys, anyway, lemme just say, I'll do this super quick. I hired—this is awful! I hired Timothy when he almost hit me in the back of a cab after a Christmas party one night. He actually took a swing at me. And it was that day I knew I loved him."

Everyone laughed? In a somewhat horrified way.

"And I hired Jacob in part because he almost identically resembled my kid brother," Thomas said, "who has an uncontrollable temper. It turns out, guess what? So. But. The two of them, it's fair to say, are joining what might be considered the most distinguished alumni society in the world."

The two of them, Thomas said, represented what made

the business an "astonishing institution"—a "combination of intellect, drive, sensibility and, I would just say, tremendous vitality. How's that? Hey! That was a code word for insatiable sexual desire. Is that a good way to put it?" Everyone laughed. "I'd just like to say the essence of it is, the older you get, or the older I've gotten, the more I've learned is that the only thing that matters is integrity."

Trixie got up right away, during the applause. Trixie was really going to be John's official boss now.

"I just wanted to say that I really wanted this to be also a celebration of the last six months of all of us working together," she said, "and working so hard for Timothy, and for Jacob. I think a lot of us experienced—they plucked us out of some weird—we met them in a bar!" She had met Timothy years and years before she'd worked there. "A lot of our connections are through these two, and then they brought us to Thomas. I love working for you guys together, you're a great team, and you're going to do great in the future, and I'm really excited for you." Then everyone went out in the cold to smoke. Good-bye! everyone said. Good-bye, good-bye!

JOHN HAD A good-bye party of his own, at the Phoenix, because he was going overseas, early in the morning, for a week. Fred had paid for a cheap ticket for him to visit. His flight left at nine a.m., from an airport pretty far away, which meant he'd have to get up at five thirty a.m. or so. He hadn't packed. He wasn't sure where his passport was either.

"Do you have to show your passport both ways?" he'd asked Sally earlier at the office.

"Um . . . ," she said. He did; passports were the international identification required to travel between countries.

Edward was going back to his parents' house, because of course he wouldn't be caught dead in the apartment without John.

Chad was there, and he was a little crazy, all wound up. Everyone was smoking outside.

"Aren't you actually going so as to get away from the insane filth?" Chad asked Edward. He said something about how the bathtub was so disgusting.

"I can hear you, it's not like you're three hundred feet away," John said, and gave him a look.

Kevin was there, and though he was scruffy, he'd shaved his mustache off, which was a shame. Kevin was trying to figure out, for his obsessed boss, how to get more people to look at their new website. No idea!

"You should take a Tic Tac," John said. He meant Adderall. Chad said, wow, no, I'm so insanely well rested, I don't need any focus, I don't actually do anything all day.

Chad was doing fine with just tutoring a couple days a week and working very part time at home for John's company. But that didn't fill all his days. He really wasn't doing anything right now. He didn't really get out of bed, not even to make it into the living room. Like he'd get to the living room finally, and then it was sunset. He wasn't even watching TV all day, just sort of idly reading sometimes, or staring into the computer.

Something was in the air. Pretty much everyone had grown a beard, even Jason, who looked healthy—his face had gotten a little scruffy as a contrast with the shaved head.

Jason had done something a few hours earlier that made him feel weird. He'd picked up a guy online and had coffee with him and then had invited him back to the office, where they'd totally had sex. The guy was really into that. The guy said to Jason, "This is so hot."

But instead of picking the guy up on Manhunt or Craigslist, he'd used Grindr, a program on his phone.

"It makes Manhunt look like two cups and a string," John said.

Grindr was a program that ran on only very elaborate telephones. When you turned it on, it just showed a grid of pictures of guys. They would have a little green icon if they were actually online right then; otherwise, they'd have been recently online. And because everyone was on their phone, they could be located, so it would show you how far away everyone was. So when Jason turned it on, and there were all these guys, good-looking too, who were like 65 and 132 and 332 feet away. It was like in a popular movie from a while back called *Aliens*, where people on this other planet built a tracking device and attached it to their guns so that they could track the movement of terrifying monsters. But this was for sex.

"I guess you shouldn't look a gift butthole in the . . . butthole?" Edward said. "But . . ." It made him feel old-fashioned.

"I'm a serial monogamist," Edward said.

Jason had been using it for only two weeks and already he felt like he should get rid of it. Like it was bad for him. And bad for everyone. Just bad. Mostly there was too much total information awareness to it.

EDWARD HAD A lot of time to think while John was gone. He knew zero people who had died basically, although his grandparents were both dead. Having both your parents die while you're still essentially a child was the very definition of bad luck, he thought. But just because unlucky things had happened, that doesn't mean they'd continue to happen, Edward thought, and that had become a major, if rarely expressed, part of John's self-conception. Edward thought John had a notion that other people were likely to die surprisingly. That's why he wasn't good about looking after his health and did things like postponing medical tests. But also Edward thought that people bent over backward to help John.

Edward's sister quit her job to take an unpaid internship—she was the same age as John—and Edward wondered, how are you going to afford this? And she was really evasive. Maybe her boyfriend was helping her out, or their parents were. He was glad she'd quit. In her industry—well, in every industry now, he thought—it had become fully institutionalized that people were treated as completely disposable. Useful until you were broken, and then you were trash to be taken out. Edward on some level wanted John to just quit his job, even though he knew that was crazy, and then where would the two of them be? Edward didn't know if it was luck or not, but Edward saw that John had all these strong connections and people wanted to help him. Also he thought that John had some magnetism, where people looked at him and wanted to take him in. There was something in his face. He was feckless, but it seemed to work for him.

A while back, Edward had accidentally come across one

of John's student loan bills. It freaked him out. At least they can't repossess your education, he thought.

The student loan thing is just kicking a can down the road; those people should all be put in jail, he thought. All the private lenders just managed to piggyback on a person—and you can't declare bankruptcy?

Edward made a point of being in the apartment only when John was there, even though it was kind of a pain. He knew John's cousin and liked him, but still, sometimes you just wanted to be alone. It was a tiny space, and even if you love the intruder, there comes a time when you remember that person is watching cable, which costs money, so it's time for him to put a quarter in the slot. Though of course the roommate's girlfriend was home all the time too.

Also he wanted to be independent. But it would be bad to step backward. To get his own apartment would be regressing. There would be weird negotiations, like: Are you sleeping over? How would you parse out your time? Those kind of discussions would become a necessity. But also Edward knew that John would never ever sleep anywhere else. Edward had stayed everywhere, and he'd had to basically beg John to come along. Plus John was kind of afraid of cats. Once when Edward was house-sitting at this place with this little tiny kitten, John was basically terrified every time it moved. John was a homebody and also a bit of a charming control freak; he enjoyed playing on his own turf.

Anyway the whole thing was like the dead shark thing from *Annie Hall*, Edward thought: The relationship had to keep moving or else it died.

CHAD MET AN art history senior who attended one of the good local colleges. He had a ridiculous name! Branford Loverford Covington. He's so beautiful, Chad said. Gorgeously beautiful.

They met in real life. Branford was friends with Dieter, from John's office. They had all been at the Phoenix one night, again, and then Branford emailed Chad to follow up after, and they became museum buddies. That meant that they were friends who went to museums together.

Chad made it clear that he lived with his partner. I would like to be friends, Chad said to him. It's very hard, Chad thought. In his head, when Mariel Hemingway and Woody Allen were at that gallery in *Manhattan*, that's how Chad felt about himself, though he wasn't as funny as Woody Allen. But he felt like the old creepy man leaning on the sprightly young gorgeous person. He was too young to feel old and creepy! But there he was, feeling disgusting under Branford's clear gaze.

Branford's parents disapproved of his lifestyle, living in the City, studying high-minded things! They were the sort of family that had never doubted its quality, its validity. They were the kind of family that kept recycling the same names for their children, generation after generation. They'd already gotten it right the first time.

Branford and Chad went to a show about the Bauhaus together. They had intellectual conversations, about ideas and life and love and history and death. It's a peculiar kind of heartbreak to be in love with someone and to feel that flush of infatuation with someone else. Branford's gravity was crushing, and Chad wanted to let go and throw himself at him.

EDWARD HAD ONCE asked John if John ever saw a future where he cleaned up a little bit. And John was like, no, I'll just get a cleaning lady.

There is a little bit of insanity that creeps into your life because of filth. Like one day Edward couldn't find his Nintendo game. So he literally did nothing. He sat in the apartment while the roommate was out and twiddled his thumbs. Edward spent a lot of time feeling sorry for himself. He thought about things and worried. Like, he owed Aric a lot of money, he thought. Or maybe he didn't? He didn't know how to approach it. He didn't know if he actually had to pay it or not. The thing was that he felt like he owed something.

Edward thought the Internet had destroyed his brain in the last two years. In part he thought it was chat. It was the closest thing to telepathy. He could beam any thought into other people's minds. And he was faster, more articulate, funnier than in person, or he thought so. He taught himself to program in BASIC when he was eight, but instead of using it for anything interesting, he made little games. And he liked playing those text games, which taught him to type and prepared him for the world of the Internet that was to come, when chat, suddenly, became omnipresent. One thing that happened was that things came easy when he was young, and then when things didn't come easy anymore, he didn't know how to try, how to study, how to learn. Also having a laptop meant you never had to be away from the Internet for long. Everywhere had Internet now. If he could burn the Internet down, he thought he'd be happy. He thought it had physically changed the way his brain worked. He couldn't even watch TV without a computer on his lap, or unless he was really stoned, or preferably both. He was too poor to smoke too much pot. Though he'd got some recently.

He had one hundred dollars, so he'd gone out and bought some. He really only liked smoking pot alone. He just wanted to watch *Oprah* and smoke pot, but didn't want to talk to anyone. Some guy took him to some other guy's apartment and he didn't even know who was selling it. John had slept with one of the guys once, and it was very awkward and he gave the guy the money and took a smaller bag and the guy was like, you can take the bigger bag, and so Edward spent seventy dollars and got what seemed like a lot. And he gave a lot of it away. He did feel bad that he'd introduced John to pot. John was pretty clean when Edward met him. He smoked too many cigarettes—well, so did Edward—but also cigarettes were probably his number-one financial expenditure. He wouldn't go a day without buying cigarettes no matter how broke he was.

Edward's friendship circle had really changed. Part of it was breaking up with Aric. And Jason's ex, who'd been one of Edward's closest friends, he was still off on the other coast. Another friend had moved to another state to go to grad school. And moving home, all the endless back and forth, the house-sitting, it had disrupted other friendships. So more and more Edward was hanging out with John's friends, though at least Jason bridged that gap, as their friend. But he felt a need to branch out on his own. Also he couldn't stand being near John and Chad. He liked them both. But together they had this whole thing—last time he'd seen them they were flailing around so much that John hit Edward in the face on accident. But it was all of a piece. Edward thought he'd lost a lot of ground in terms of his independence. He'd been with Aric since he was twenty-two. He thought he'd missed out on developing certain skills. And so his natural instinct was to gravitate very close to one person and—well, on the other hand, it was fun. But it felt a little bit dire. Edward would feel bad if John stayed home all the time, but that is what he wanted. If they didn't lay out the terms of what they were doing, fights ensued. John tended to double-book. Sometimes triple-book. John piled more and more people into every possible occasion. Edward thought John fancied himself this very spontaneous person who would go where the night took him. And he did, except he was hemmed in by the wall of conflicting plans he'd make every night.

Getting out of all of this could be accomplished by Edward getting an apartment. That would be pretty hard to do when he had only thirty dollars left of that hundred.

IT WAS A long week that John was gone. Edward stewed at his parents' house. He realized he had very mixed feelings about cohabitating, so he wanted to pretend that he wasn't actually doing so in as many ways as possible.

Before he left, John had again offered to make him keys. And Edward said, but doesn't that big key cost like forty dollars to duplicate? And John said, oh okay, never mind.

Edward worried that their whole relationship would happen as fast as it already had. That they'd burn through and in a year it'd be done. John didn't worry at all though, so he said. Don't worry about it, he always said. Enjoy yourself. Don't worry about it. It was a wall of "don't worry." One day they'd had a little fight over nothing, basically, and Edward explained that he'd made these extrapolations, that like, no, the reason this tiny thing bothers me is that he anticipated being with John a really long time. So Edward was thinking his whole life he'd never get to choose what they were going to watch on TV. And that Edward was thinking that way freaked John out a little bit. At least so Edward thought.

Edward could wedge himself into a cozy feedback loop, amplifying problems—or nonproblems—by thinking too much. Edward told John to choose just one thing that Edward was interested in and then, going forward, he should pretend to be also interested in it. Because so far if there were two choices of what was on TV, something that Edward would like and anything else, it was always anything else.

People are just so annoying, was what Edward thought.

Even people you love are annoying. The good news is that things could get worked out in sex, even in ways you didn't realize maybe. Even though Edward realized he'd never have sex as much as he did with his boyfriend his sophomore year of college, when they basically blew off a semester in order to have sex. Though maybe it would help if there was more of a working bed at John's apartment? Still it was romantic, as they did get a bit huddled up in its broken embrace.

WHEN JOHN FINALLY returned from overseas to another, nearer country—at this time, it was often cheaper, bizarrely, to fly to multiple destinations in the airplanes than to fly directly from point to point—John found out his phone didn't work anymore. He'd been putting the phone company off for a long time again, and the phone no longer had service.

But there was Internet at the airport, so he went online and Jason was there. And Jason wrote, oh my God, I met the hot transit reporter from the local TV news station, he's so hot. And didn't even ask about how the trip was.

So John hadn't missed anything in a week.

The bars were amazing overseas. And the museums too. Timothy had warned him in advance to order mixed drinks to save money, but this was incorrect advice.

Everyone over there drank Jack Daniels, for some reason, but it was much more expensive than beer. He arrived with 350 dollars, 100 dollars of which was borrowed from Edward, improbably. That came to about 200 units in this other currency. This was gone by the weekend, four days in. Cigarettes were only 2.40 units or so, and pints of beer were 1 unit.

The first two nights, John and Fred hit the bars pretty hard. On Saturday night, *Don't Look Now,* starring Julie Christie and Donald Sutherland, was playing at the local theater at midnight. So they went to the hot bar by Fred's house and had a couple drinks; then midnight rolled around. There was almost no one in the theater.

But suddenly there was a man with a microphone. "I know most of you here," he said, "except for a couple of you, and the theater has very graciously allowed me, on the occasion of my fiftieth birthday, to screen my favorite movie in my favorite theater." The movie was incredible. The evening was incredible. Half a century! And after, John and Fred breezed back into the bar with their hand stamps, past the huge line, to be with the young men again.

The big difference that John could see between the City and overseas was that all the bars over there were dance bars, and everyone danced. Fred had gone boy crazy while living there, John found. He had three friends. One was a hot boy from the hinterlands who was basically Fred's Edward: He'd been in a relationship for nearly five years, and most likely was not available. Or maybe so! And everywhere they went, Fred was like, whipping around, looking at boys. And yes, okay, they were all very attractive, John thought . . . and yet John wasn't tempted. Nothing happened. The accents were beginning to give him a headache. Well. One particularly aggressive boy threw himself on John and began kissing him vigorously. Still John arrived safe, and unsullied, at home near the City, every penny spent, without even the money to get from the airport to his house.

THE NEW BOSS fired John's boss Trixie.

We need your salary to pay other people more money, is what her boss said.

John felt, as much as he could still feel about work, bad. He was out of the office when it happened. He and other people in the office exchanged tiny text messages that said things like "yikes."

THE YEAR, IT ended. John's room—John and Edward's room?—was filthier than ever.

There were, on his desk, a few notes from the state,

about that tax issue from a few years back, before John started working at a real job. They still wanted 417.11 dollars.

Deeper in the drawer: a phone bill, due October 8, with a total due of 271.19 dollars, with a minimum payment of 151.65.

A bill from Callen-Lorde health services, regarding a doctor's visit. The visit cost 200 dollars, but was offset by a sliding scale discount of 130, and he'd paid 25 at the time, so they wanted 45 more.

There was a letter from I.C. System Inc. of St. Paul–Minneapolis, on behalf of Jason Hudson, DDS, for a dentist bill in the amount of 461.93 dollars.

There was a letter from NYU Langone Medical Center regarding a doctor's visit on September 23 with Dr. Lisa Kalik. The visit had cost 250 dollars, but Oxford, John's health insurance, had paid the majority of it and they now wanted to be paid 30 dollars.

There was a letter from Cynthia MacKay, MD, an ophthalmologist, from December 28 of the last year, of a bill that was ninety days overdue. The visit had cost 175 dollars, and he owed 10.

And paystubs. At the end of the year John had received what they called "gross" pay in the amount of 43,317.43 dollars.

There was a deduction in that pay in the amount of

2,428.39 dollars, which was John's share of his partially employer-paid health insurance.

There was a deduction in the amount of 999.75 dollars for transportation—for the subway fare cards provided through his job. These unlimited ride cards cost 89 dollars a month. This discounted group version reduced his cost to 83.31 dollars a month.

So John's total income that was reported to the government for the year past was, after all this, 39,889.29 dollars.

In this, he was way ahead of a great percentage of the world at that time.

There were, speaking very roughly, 3.2 billion people with jobs in the whole world. Looking at the total world population at the time and the amount of money earned by countries all over the world, without setting aside government money, the average yearly per-person income might have been something between 6,000 and 10,000 dollars a month. The average person in the whole country, meanwhile, made something near 32,000 dollars a year, although most of those people lived in places that were far less expensive than the City.

Of that 39,889.29 dollars, John had to give some of that away. There was also some money kept back from him for paying into the country's Social Security program, which provided a modest monthly income for the disabled and the elderly.

So they set aside, throughout this year, 2,473.14 dollars for Social Security, and also an estimated federal tax payment of 3,692.48 dollars, and a payment to Medicare, which provided health services to the poor, of 578.39 dollars, and also local taxes were withheld in the amount of 1,113.08 dollars.

After all that, he was down to 74 percent of his total pay: 32,032.20 dollars, or 2,669.35 a month.

THE MAYOR, AS required, filed his final reports for the year. It turned out he had spent 108 million dollars of his own money on his third-term reelection campaign.

His challenger had been able to get only about 10 million dollars together to spend, and even so had come up short by only 50,597 votes.

The Mayor wouldn't miss the money. Or so it was easy to think. A funny thing about money was that, even when you had a lot, even when the perspective skewed so wildly that you could purchase in cash things that cost millions of dollars, when you could walk into a building and write a check for the building itself, or walk into an art gallery or a car showroom and take anything or everything you wanted, or spend 20 million dollars on a renovation of one of your secondary homes, it was often true that the feeling of parting with money was just the same for everyone, rich or poor.

CHAD AND DIEGO hadn't seen each other in a couple of nights. Chad was out a lot. Diego said to Chad finally, "You know you're not single anymore, right?"

AT WORK, THEY weren't necessarily lying when they'd told Trixie that they needed her salary for other uses. John was getting a raise. It didn't mean they had to fire her, but still.

Each of John's paychecks would go up 230 dollars, for a total of 460 more dollars a month. So he'd be making 2,700 a month.

It wasn't going to change everything, exactly, but John thought he could live like, he said, a human being. Like he could do things now. If he wanted to buy socks, he could. And he would get haircuts.

And he thought Edward would be getting a paycheck soon too, maybe, from somewhere. Their first line item was to get a new bed.

The big picture of the raise, it's incredible, John thought. And he would start paying off his other government debts again. Maybe 150 a month. He could, and he wanted to, do 150 dollars.

He was actually excited.

So say that was 675 each week. So, after he paid his basic monthly agreements of about 1,315 dollars, for almost exactly half his income, he'd be left with between 44 and 46 each day to spend on other things.

That would make all the difference.

John's cousin was applying to professional schools. He had gotten into a very fancy one that was far from the City. So he'd be leaving pretty soon, most likely. John fantasized about keeping his little apartment with Edward. And they'd have one room for sleeping, and then the public room for cooking and eating and watching TV and socializing, and then a third room, which had been his cousin's, for working or reading or thinking. Edward would be able to afford half of the rent himself soon, John thought. Maybe!

Meanwhile Edward was looking at getting some cheap deal on some squatted apartment in the City, which John didn't like, and it sounded all kinds of dubious. Honestly, this was probably just another thing that Edward talked about. He talked about a lot of things, and few of them happened. John thought if he just got a nicer bed, Edward would just stay put, finally, for once.

Problem was, John thought he'd have gotten his raise in his last check but he hadn't, and blammo, he'd run out of money for five days.

In the week before the raise, Sally and another friend at work had bought him lunch, and then a friend had bought him dinner. Then on Friday, John planned to spend fifteen dollars and get a haircut.

John called Edward to say hi.

Edward was all comfortable at his parents', eating a pizza with Gruyère, a pricey cheese. He had a glass of wine, a Chardonnay.

John was hungry and tired and maybe a little bit drunk.

People lived to suit their means. They expanded; money would make their costs grow. If you had a lot of money, it found things to do and it kept you busy, and when you stopped to pull back and look at it all, suddenly you were spending nearly all your money and you didn't know why.

What's the first thing you're going to buy when you get your check on Friday? Edward asked.

Socks, John said. I really need socks.

He was actually a little annoyed.

Later that week Edward planned to get John some dinner sent through the Internet, and he'd pay for it with his mother's credit card.

It was maybe going to be John's last broke Thursday, maybe.

The next day John was really nice to Edward when they talked.

ON FRIDAY NIGHT, right before Edward came back, John went out with Ralph, his old friend from college, on a massive bar tour. They hadn't seen each other in ages!

They stopped here and there, Eastern Bloc, the Boiler Room, ending at the Cock.

All these bars were right by Jordan's apartment, and they met up with Jason and Jeff. Jordan and Jeff had just broken up, so John kept texting Jordan to tell him not to come to whatever bar they were in at the moment.

Everyone thought that Jeff and Jordan were more fun to go out with now that they were broken up. Jeff and Jordan, when they were together, would always get jealous, like, are you looking at that guy? What, no, I'm not!

It got late and pretty much everyone was wasted. Every once in a while, Jason was like, "Who wants a Tic Tac?"

They breezed past the doorwoman at the Cock. Eventually John went down to the basement to pee, and it was wall-to-wall guys down there. One guy having sex locked eyes with John as John squeezed by.

John went back upstairs and grabbed Ralph, all wild-eyed. "We have to get out of here," he said. Ralph was happy to. To see John so devoted to someone again, after all these years of not believing it was possible, Ralph thought it was wonderful. He came back home with John, instead of going way uptown where he lived. Ralph slept in the broken-down twin bed and John slept on the floor. At around four thirty a.m., John called Edward, who sensibly didn't answer.

In the morning John's cousin got up and went to the bathroom through the living room, passing what he assumed was Edward on the computer. When he came out of the bathroom, he realized it was Ralph. Ralph was busy meeting a guy on Adam4Adam, yet another place people met online. The guy came over and got him and drove him—in his car!—all the way uptown.

John woke up and Ralph was gone, and he opened the window into the cold hard morning and smoked a cigarette out the window. Eventually he got bundled up and went to the little coffee shop directly across the street.

He sat outside on the bench with a cup of coffee and lit a cigarette. His phone buzzed in his pants. It was Edward calling back. He was so happy to talk to him.

"You know how much snow we have here? Zero. . . . There's salt all over the ground. There's salt. I mean it was flirting with snowing last night, we were like, oh, the snow's coming. Then it just never came. . . . Um, we had quite the night last night. Well, Ralph and I started at G, then we went to get dinner at that La Lunchonette on Tenth Avenue, it was so good. Then we went to the porn shop to get lube. Then we went to Gym Bar. . . . No! That's why I was laughing. Like I don't need this shit anymore. It's really expensive. Oh my God. I mean he bought like a jug of it for forty dollars. Then we went to Gym Bar. . . .

A giant jug of lube in his pocket. But they wrapped it like, you know, like a nice French bread or something. They did a very nice job of wrapping it. . . . Then we went to Eastern Cock, where we met up with Jason and Patrick and Jeff. . . . And Patrick was so nice last night! Yeah, I was shocked. He was the nicest guy ever last night. . . . No, completely. He must be on meds. So we were at Eastern Cock, then we went to Boiler Room, where we ran into Bryan and Sam and Steve or whatever his name is. He's a total bitch. Ugh, such a bitch. Then we went to the Cock, L. O. L. Mmm-hmm. It was kind of insane. I ran out, like, terrified. I mean it was just vintage Cock. I stayed in the front and was dancing and then I had to go to the bathroom and it was too scary so I made Ralph leave and we just walked out and Jeff and Jason stayed behind. . . . And then Ralph slept over last night and I'm unbelievably hungover. . . . Yeah. I'll call you back. Okay? Okay. I'll call you. Alright, bye."

The wind was coming down from the north and it was very cold. The landlord's son who ran the real estate business downstairs from John's apartment came and opened up the shop. They waved. John finished up his coffee and went back inside his building and up the stairs.

That night, John was going over to dinner at Kevin's. He was looking forward to a home-cooked meal. They could be married homebodies together! They were survivors, or something.

AND THEN IN the very harshest dead of winter it was Jason's birthday. Jason was thirty years old now and that meant he was all grown up. Well, he guessed. What would change? Nothing? Jason felt like he had turned thirty ten years ago. Especially since he'd been married—at eighteen!—and all that stuff. Maybe I'm turning something less than thirty, he thought. If he'd learned anything from the writer Armistead Maupin, he thought, the one thing he'd learned is that you can't have a hot job, a hot man and a hot apartment all at the same time. He really did believe that. He felt like he'd had combinations of those three things for almost all of his life, and now the pieces were shifting but he still didn't have all of those. Maybe, thinking about it, maybe he had none of those? Although he kind of liked his apartment. And he, alone among his friends, liked his job most days! But he definitely did not have a hot boyfriend.

On second thought, maybe he did not subscribe at all to this maxim. It sounded stupid.

The countrywide contagion, as the Mayor had suggested, did seem to be ending. At least, people couldn't sustain their attention on it. It wasn't that everyone had a job again though. The panic had been half real, half imaginary. Plenty of companies and owners survived just fine. Some even prospered. It was the results of the panic that were all real.

And so the people who had jobs felt like they'd lived by their wits, and John felt this way most times. Or they felt they'd escaped by luck, and Edward felt this way sometimes—except when he felt he hadn't escaped. And there were people who felt they'd escaped but only barely, and they knew it was maybe only for a bit. You could actually literally always be more poor than you were, as surprising as that might seem when you owed tens of thousands of dollars or made only a few hundred dollars or, in the City, a few thousand dollars a month.

But then, the whole point of being in this City, it turned out, was staying nimble enough to take advantage of whatever strange things the City might choose to offer to you.

Movement started. Soon enough, Trixie got a job, and then an even better job. Edward was actually soon to get a job as well, with an office and a boss who would buy him a laptop computer. His boss was, of course, a rich millionaire, just like everyone else's boss, and he would turn out to be domineering and impulsive and aggressive and perhaps crazy. But everyone was used to that in a boss by now. That was just how things were.

And soon enough, Kevin, who had gotten his current job after being laid off, would get laid off again by John's owner's cousin. He was more panicked by this second job loss than he would have thought he might have been. Surviving the first one was one thing. But doing it again? How disposable could one person be? he thought.

And Jason took up a hot and heavy affair with a really sweet guy that John had once dated. So, for a while, Jason actually did have a great apartment, a great job and a great boyfriend all at once. It turned out to not be as amazing as it was supposed to be.

Actually, almost all of everything changed after this night. Sally was the last of everyone they knew to quit their office. She felt like the last passenger stepping off a sinking ship and into the lifeboats. She was the last because, just before that, John left the company too, to go work for a much-bigger company—where their old boss Thomas was the new boss. Thomas's new boss, that company's owner, was of course an extravagantly wealthy man, just like the last boss, just like everyone else's boss, but he was very old and secretive. And while the company was enormously successful, and no one was sure what would happen when he died, still, it felt like some kind of security.

Also John's cousin did move out to go to school, and Edward did finally accept a key to the apartment.

And something else happened. It wasn't that everyone stopped being friends after this one last night. They were still friends, after so much; they just weren't so piled up together. It was part of the end of being young, or it was part of it having been the strangest, most exhausting year. Or it had just been a moment. After this, whole weekends, and then whole weeks, went by without everyone hanging out.

THE CITY, IT changed more slowly. One thing that happened, with the Mayor's very loud support, was that it finally became legal for two men, or two women, to marry each other. That was something that some young people in love had to think about for the first time.

The funny thing about being the Mayor was that you weren't, for all the attention you got, really all that powerful. What had the Mayor done, in all his time in office? His real work wasn't in the announcements of rezoning or the opening and closing of schools—although he did shut down at least 140 schools in the City while in office—or in the little programs that were supposed to help people start small businesses. His real work was as a whisperer, a money-giver, an influencer. It was in the giving away of his endless supply of money, and in his rich-person-to-rich-person conversations, that he did his most important work. In private, he kept other rich people's companies in the City—not that they would leave the City anyway. But from time to time, a company would pretend that it was leaving the City for someplace less expensive, and the Mayor would make sure they received tax breaks and other considerations, and so the company would stay. Well, the company itself would stay: But it would hire more workers, who worked for less money, in cheaper parts of the country or the world.

By its nature, the City gained back the number of jobs that it had lost, and then made more. But really they were only jobs for some people. In the month the Mayor announced his very first candidacy, the rate of unemployment in the City—the percentage of working people who wanted and did not have a job—was 5.3 percent. In the month that he won his third term, it was 9.8 percent. That rate never really receded significantly while he was the Mayor.

The City's owners just had access to more people than they needed. A whole class of people had been created. They were unwanted: They weren't needed as workers, and they were barely needed as consumers. Also if they weren't workers, then they weren't in a position to be consumers. Not enough money ran through them.

Across the whole country, the jobs that had for some time engaged people who were not rich quite literally vanished. Those jobs were replaced with either no job at all, or with quite low-paying work. So in the future, some people might climb up out of this class. But most would not.

It wasn't like this was a thing that wasn't talked about. Everyone knew about it! But it wasn't like anyone had the responsibility of just giving people jobs. It wasn't anyone's problem, and so it was no one's problem. It wasn't in anyone's interest to change this, which also must have meant it was in someone's interest to not change this.

The City Council, at least, finally decided that they should pass a law to forbid businesses from discriminating against the unemployed during hiring. Businesses wouldn't even be allowed to advertise that candidates had to be currently employed.

But the Mayor scoffed at this. He said that he thought this would be bad for business.

Before the Mayor left office, a 2,415-square-foot three-bedroom apartment in the building that bore his name sold for thirteen and a half million dollars. That apartment had most recently sold for just a bit more than five million dollars. That was just back at the beginning of the Mayor's second term. Having money was really quite magical.

JASON'S THIRTIETH BIRTHDAY party was held at this bizarre place in the bottom of the City, down at sea level,
just off the water, for now, where all the great fabled
finance companies had their buildings, where all the
money came and went. The place was clearly a home to
gangster parties, or maybe the kind of place that businessmen went to meet women who weren't their wives.
Everything outside was blue-gray and cold, and the stone
of all the buildings felt thick and wet and old. Inside it
was like being in a secret city inside the City. It was enormous, on a second floor, all mirrored and crazy and uncomfortable, with security men who had guns.

Everyone was there.

There were plenty of problems. Jason was throwing
the party with one of his best friends, Emma, and all her
cool-haired girlfriends were there, and they were pretty
dramatic. The party was a huge hysterical success, a real
mess. There was a screaming match between the women
and the security guards at one point. A guy had gone
into the women's room to help Emma's girlfriend, who
was busy vomiting outrageously, and the security guard
freaked out.

John had a flask in his tattered old coat, the same coat
as last winter, and he'd sneak sips from the flask. Outside
he'd smoke in his thin coat; it was cold and you could

see straight down out to the harbor, like staring into the future. He'd get a new coat next winter.

The boy who'd introduced Edward and John came downstairs outside to bum a smoke. "He's such a cig pig," Jason said, with fondness.

Everyone got drunk. The new year was aging oddly. Edward needled John about how John's friends all thought Edward was a fishwife. Don't worry about it, dolly, John said to Edward. Edward did worry, quite a lot, but in time he'd try to get over it.

Ralph was on the dance floor. He was in good spirits, but, he told everyone, he was going to maybe be homeless for a couple of weeks after his roommate situation had suddenly blown up.

At this party, amazingly, Jordan, John's ex, started kissing Tyler Flowers. The next morning, Jordan would call and text John like a thousand times. No one even knew why they'd invited Tyler! Old habits. Jordan and Tyler totally hadn't slept together, Jordan swore to John. He was sorry!

John could not care less. Why had he been after Tyler Flowers again? What a strange, strange year. You're welcome to Tyler Flowers, he said—you're all welcome to him.

Still at the party, as it got late, Chad sat at a table in

a mirrored hallway, his head literally in his hands. Boys were sashaying up and down the hallway. He was thinking about Branford. He was thinking about leaving Diego. He definitely also didn't think he should leave Diego under any circumstances. He was thinking about sleeping with Branford. He was all tied up. John and Edward came and sat at his table. There were dozens of reflections of them from all these strange angles, all surrounding Chad. Edward was sitting on John's lap. Would Chad or wouldn't Chad? Would he or wouldn't he? Throw it all away, start over, he wasn't even sure, was it an obsession or something else, or what were these feelings? Could he have a secret affair? That hadn't worked out so well for Edward. Or wait: It had, actually! For Edward. But not for Edward's boyfriend. Would he or wouldn't he? Tonight, at least, he thought it was very likely that he would.

John and Edward listened to this talk for a while. Then Edward got off John's lap, and they went and danced, with everyone they knew around them in this magnificent hideout all tucked away in this City of limitless strangeness. No one would ever find them all there even if the search went on for years. It got very late, or very early, and John and Edward, all wrung out and laughing, went home to be alone together while they could.

ACKNOWLEDGMENTS

IN ORDER: Jacqueline Miller Thomason, Susan Farm-brough, Philo Hagen, Dr. Robert Wolski, Peter Butler, Alexander Chee, Dale Peck, Leslie Harpold, Rosecrans Baldwin, Andrew Womack, Paul Ford, Jon Robin Baitz, Nick Debs, Nick Denton, Nick Philippou, Maria Russo, Elizabeth Spiers, Ariel Kaminer, Kate Aurthur, Jodi Kantor, Peter Kaplan, Suzy Hansen, Emily Gould, Tom Scocca, Sara Vilkomerson, Julia Cheiffetz, Alex Balk, David Cho, John Shankman, Carrie Frye, Ken Layne, Natasha Vargas-Cooper, Brett Sokol and Mack Scocca-Ho. Of course, Andrew's Couch. Also Cain, William James, Peregrine and Little Man. For their support, the New York Public Library, the Miami Public Library, the staff of Craft Restaurant and the unionized workers of American Airlines. PJ Mark and Barry Harbaugh. David Michael Valdez. Everyone who spoke to me for this book.

ABOUT THE AUTHOR

CHOIRE SICHA is the coproprietor of *The Awl*. A two-time editor of *Gawker,* he has written for the *New York Times* and the *Los Angeles Times* as well as a suspiciously large number of magazines exactly one time. He lives in Brooklyn.